# WHEN TURKEYS TALKED
# AND
# POLITICIANS WERE PEOPLE

# John Donaldson

**VANTAGE PRESS**
NEW YORK

Published by Vantage Press, Inc.
516 West 34th Street, New York, New York 10001

Manufactured in the United States of America
ISBN: 0-533-12948-6

Library of Congress Catalog Card No.: 98-94013

0 9 8 7 6 5 4 3 2 1

To all Spring Creekers: past, present, and future

# Contents

# Introduction

Few people were fortunate enough to have lived in Spring Creek, Pennsylvania during the 1930's. Those who did not, missed knowing a lot of wonderful and highly talented people, people like Mrs. McGee, the best whistler in Warren County; Lefty, who was better than anybody doing anything except wallpapering; and Clifford, a finer cook than they had at the Waldorf-Astoria in New York City. Never would these unlucky persons have attended such outstanding events as the Ladies Aid Society's annual talent show or the Grade School's Christmas plays. Nor is it likely they would have heard about the night the Devil came to play bridge; or how Preacher Bentley and Apostle Paul prevented the end of the world; or about the doggoned joke LR (my old man) played on the skinflint bank president.

In the stories that follow you'll become acquainted with at least a few of those wonderful people. You will also learn about some of the very outstanding events which occurred in and near Spring Creek during the 1930's. And you will hopefully get some idea of what it would have been like to have lived near the Brokenstraw Creek when politicians were people. That is, except for that slippery-tongued devil in Washington, FDR, who completely ignored the plight of poor Spring Creek farmers and storekeepers.

The stories are essentially true; however, that's not to say there are not some embellishments, additions, and alterations to be found here and there in a weak effort to add suspense, drama, and/or believability. Furthermore, many of the names are fictitious so any survivors of that era, or their relatives, won't be embarrassed by being associated in any way with this sort of book!

The remainder of this introduction is about the town of Spring Creek which, you probably already know, is a small town straddling the Brokenstraw Creek in the northwest corner of Pennsylvania. For those interested in knowing exactly where it is located, it's at the bottom of the Blue Eye Hill and three miles north of West Spring Creek in one direction; in the other, it's exactly half-way between Garland and Corry.

Chances are you never travelled through Spring Creek during the 1930's because not many people did. The road from Corry to Garland wasn't paved and was therefore muddy or covered with snow most of the year. However, if you had passed through back then, you would have seen that while Spring Creek wasn't a very big place, it was a very busy one because of all the important buildings.

Each and every day of the week (Sundays were no exception), the Spring Creek area farmers brought their cans of milk to the **Milk Plant.** From earlier than six in the morning until half past nine or ten o'clock, their old trucks and horses- or tractor-drawn wagons rattled through town and lined up in the milk plant driveway. When their turn came to unload, the milk in the cans was checked for flies and cream. Flies were not allowed, but the more cream there was the more the farmer got paid. The milk from the cans with no flies was poured into a tank, weighed and pumped through coolers and separators where it was turned into cream and skim milk. The cream went to a waiting refrigerated railroad tank car and was sent all the way to Philadelphia where people could afford it. The skim milk, which wasn't worth much, was dried on a long, large, revolving steam-heated stainless steel drum, put in burlap bags and sold back cheap to the farmers for pig and cow feed. (Today it would be sold at full price to people who prefer "fat free" milk.)

After the farmers collected their empty, steam-cleaned cans from the long roller conveyor outside the milk plant, they would often as not go over to Uncle Lon's **Feed Mill.** At the feed mill they bought 100-pound bags of grain for their cows, horses, pigs, and chickens. Some bags were printed with flowers so the farmers' wives could use them to make dresses. In the fall, the farmers would have what they had grown during the summer—wheat, rye, oats, corn, and whatever—ground into grain. In the spring they bought big bags of seeds, of the same

stuff which they would plant, knowing full well the growing season was going to be either too wet or too dry.

Whether or not they stopped in at the Feed Mill, most of the farmers always visited LR's **General Store** before heading home (except Sundays, when the store was closed). In case you don't know much about general stores, they came before supermarkets and shopping malls, but instead of having to go from one place to another, everything you could possibly need was bought under one roof and usually in one room. A shopping list might include meat and groceries, clothes, shoes, boots, pots, dishes, barbed wire, tar paper, nails, bolts, chewing tobacco, medicine for folks or animals, paint, guns, fishing poles and knives, dresses, and pocket watches. As well as many other things. Every item bought was carefully listed on the store bill which at least some of the farmers paid some of at the end of the month, when they got their milk check from the Milk Plant.

The **Community Building** was where people voted, had wedding receptions, political rallies, and family reunions. Many notable social events were held there including the annual Spring Creek Spring Bazaar, the annual talent show, the annual Hunters' Pancake Supper, the annual Fishermen's Pancake Breakfast, several Box Socials, Ladies Aid meetings and Friday night square dances. Some of those events might have been put on at the church except the church didn't have a kitchen, didn't allow dancing, and didn't want anything to do with alcohol, tobacco or politicians.

Kids from Spring Creek and the surrounding farms attended grades 1 through 8 at **The Spring Creek Grade School**. Grades one, two, and three were in the Little Room; the fourth, fifth, and sixth grades in the Middle Room, and the big kids in the seventh and eighth were upstairs in the Big Room. Each room had one teacher and was heated by one wood stove. Water came from an outside pump when it wasn't frozen. To go to the bathroom, you had to put up your hand to get permission, then go outside to either the boys' or girls' backhouse, depending on which gender you were. The toilets didn't freeze but whoever was using them during the winter months did.

About the last place farm animals wanted to visit was Uncle Mac's **Slaughterhouse** The slaughterhouse was where calves, cows, sheep, goats, pigs, and chickens were brought to be converted mostly into things people ate. Cow and sheep hides could eventually end up being worn or walked in, and pigskins might become a football, but mostly it was for the meat that animals met their end in the slaughterhouse. Inside the slaughterhouse were benches for folks who wanted to watch the proceedings. A short distance up a road in back of the slaughterhouse was the slaughterhouse dump. Here's where parts of animals that most people didn't want to eat—heads, ears, insides, hooves, etc.—were deposited for buzzards, dogs and foxes to fight over.

**The Blacksmith's Shop** was where you learned that when iron was heated until it turned orange it could be bent, twisted, pounded flat or made into hoops and rings. That's how Blacksmith John repaired horse shoes, wagon wheel rims, plows, tractors and other stuff for farmers. To get the iron soft enough it was held in long tongs over a charcoal fire in a big cement box. By turning the big round black "wind crank" outside the cement box, air was blown into the fire to make it hotter. Blacksmith John would also fix things for kids, broken trikes, bikes, sled runners and such, and you could work off your bill by spending a certain amount of time turning the wind crank.

A skyscraper three stories high, the **Old Cold Storage Building** was the tallest brick building in downtown Spring Creek. The other downtown skyscraper, the General Store, had only two stories. Something a lot of people may not know is that the cold storage building was the tallest brick building in all of Spring Creek Township! Before electricity and refrigerators came to the area, meat from the slaughterhouse had been kept cold there in corklined rooms cooled with dry ice.

All day long, Monday through Saturday, Mr. Johnson sat at a desk in the vestibule at the front of **The Depot**. From there he could see up and down tracks and use his telegraph to let the depots in the next towns know when trains came and went. Or when to stop and pick up a package or a passenger, which wasn't too often. Mr. Bates was there to sell tickets but hardly anybody bought any, which is why Mr. Johnson didn't stop many trains.

Mrs. Johnson was about the only person who went on the train frequently, because she got to go free of charge.

The **Congregational Church** was the only church in town so most of the Spring Creekers who went to church every Sunday were Congregationalists. The main excuse used by folks who didn't go to church regularly was they were not Congregationalists. Even though there weren't many regular parishioners, the church was a bustling place, and not just on Sundays either. Weddings, funerals, Wednesday night services, Saturday morning Bible School, choir practice, the annual Christmas plays and Easter pageants, Mothers' Day programs and special church deacon meetings were some of the things that happened there in addition to Sunday School and two services every Sunday.

Several of these played major roles in some of the following stories. The cold storage building is featured in both *The Night the Devil Came to Play Bridge* and *The Great Garbage Ambush*. It was at the church where *Preacher Bentley* and *Apostle Paul* managed to keep the world from coming to an end, and the community building was where Grampa Charlie and I won first prize at the talent show.

# WHEN TURKEYS TALKED
## AND
# POLITICIANS WERE PEOPLE

# Prologue: DOA

Thursday afternoons Corry doctors played golf at the Corry Country Club. Probably Doctor Gilly was thinking about golf in July, 1928, that Thursday afternoon when he pronounced the newest Spring Creek resident dead on arrival. Just because the little fellow was gray and not breathing.

Nurses didn't get time off for golf, ergo the nurse on duty wasn't preoccupied with thoughts of niblicks, pars or bogeys, so she knew Doctor Gilly had made a bad call. Hoisting the baby by his little gray legs, the nurse smacked his little gray bottom until it turned pink. Observing that and hearing the baby's feeble squawks, the doctor proffered a second opinion telling the nurse it was possible the baby boy wasn't dead after all!

Eleven months later the same Doctor Gilly received an emergency phone call from the parents of the same baby boy. They were alarmed because the little fellow was gasping for breath and fast turning back to his original shade of gray. By coincidence, this also occurred on a Thursday and the call reached Dr. Gilly just as he was leaving for his weekly round of golf. Acquiescing to the Hippocratic oath, the doctor detoured through Spring Creek on his way to the country club.

After a somewhat hurried examination, Dr. Gilly told the parents their little boy had pneumonia. That was his good news. The bad news was it was such an advanced case it was quite beyond where much could be done about it.

Surely, it was Divine Intervention which placed the baby's uncle, Mac, at the scene, because on this occasion it was he who recognized the doctor's bad call. Mac wasn't a moonshiner, but he was a good customer of the Grady brothers who were moonshiners. Prohibition disallowed owning whiskey, but Mac, for

1

medicinal purposes, always carried somewhere on his six-foot-three person a good-sized flask of moonshine. From years of experience he knew and appreciated the curative powers of moonshine for toothaches, sore throats, heartburn, the common cold, bloat, and many other maladies. Consequently, Mac suggested to the distressed parents that a little moonshine might get their baby to breathe once more. Being a Congregational Church deacon lady, the boy's mother didn't think much of the idea. His father, being Scotch-Irish, believed it might be a waste of good moonshine. Doctor Gilly, also Scotch-Irish, agreed with the father. Nevertheless, Mac won them over with the argument, "It might bring the boy around, and if it doesn't, he'll at least go out happy."

Two teaspoons were poured down the baby's constricted throat and he began to gag and sputter. Two more caused him to sneeze and cough. Another two and his breathing and color began to improve considerably. Two final teaspoons and the little lad opened his eyes, smiled for a moment, then fell asleep.

Of course, Mac and the parents were delighted with this miraculous recovery. As a matter of fact, so was Dr. Gilly, believing he'd discovered the long sought-after cure for pneumonia. Seventy years later the little fellow, now an old fellow, is delighted he's still around to tell about Dr. Gilly's bad calls.

# One

## When Politicians Were People

LR and Uncle Glen owned the general store in Spring Creek, so they belonged to the Republican Party. President Roosevelt was a Democrat and they knew Roosevelt's New Deal was a bad deal because he was giving away too much money to poor people and not enough to poor store owners and poor farmers who couldn't pay their store bills. Because Uncle Glen was also Spring Creek's postmaster and received a government check every month, he never talked much about politics. LR, on the other hand, did. LR would tell folks just what he thought, especially the poor ones whom LR was certain weren't anywhere near as poor as they had indicated to Mr. Roosevelt.

For quite a few years after Mr. Roosevelt became president in 1932, Spring Creekers who got relief checks and food stamps every month tended to disagree with LR. The same situation existed with the ones who had jobs in the Works Project Administration, called the WPA. President Roosevelt had invented the WPA, and people who worked for it were supposed to fix roads, build bridges, paint pictures, etc. It took so many of them so long to get anything done that Republicans said WPA stood for "We Poke Along."

Most Spring Creek Township farmers were dairy farmers and they didn't much like what LR said about President Roosevelt either. They knew for a fact it was Mr. Herbert Hoover, the president before Mr. Roosevelt, who'd caused the Great Depression. They knew it for a fact because Mr. Roosevelt had said so when he was running against Mr. Hoover in the election.

Every morning and evening somewhere around seven o'clock the Pennsylvania Railroad's Evening Flier rumbled through Spring Creek, and every morning and evening, except

3

Sundays, a U.S. mail bag was thrown out the mail car door, skidding to a stop on the cinders in front of the old depot. Postmaster Uncle Glen paid Mr. Bates good money to fetch the bags up to the post office, which was at the back end of the store just past the butcher block. While Uncle Glen sorted out the letters, catalogues and relief checks, quite a few men loafed around in the store waiting to get their mail. This was a good time for LR to argue about how Roosevelt was getting the country so far into debt we'd have to sell it back to the Indians or maybe England. Being half Irish, LR was a good talker, therefore it wasn't very long before quite a few of the loafers, even ones getting paid for doing nothing, began to agree with LR that the Great Depression wasn't going away like Roosevelt claimed it was.

When farmers came to buy groceries, LR also told them just what he thought about Roosevelt. He declared that Roosevelt's announcement the day he took office, "We have nothing to fear but fear itself," was nothing but a bunch of bull crap. LR claimed what people ought to be really afraid of was that if the government didn't get around pretty soon to doing something for the farmers, it wouldn't be long before nobody'd have anything to eat! It took awhile but eventually most of the farmers started to believe LR was hitting the nail right on the head.

Spring Creek Township is in Warren County. Down in the country seat of Warren Borough, LR got to be known by the County Republican Party people for the way he was able to talk the Democrats around Spring Creek into changing the way they thought about things. This, in turn, brought LR to the attention of Republican big-wigs all the way down in the state capital, Harrisburg. Once in a while, some of those Harrisburg politicians would drive to Warren County to hunt deer or fish for trout, and when they went through Spring Creek, they'd as often as not stop in at the store to say hello to LR.

When they came in LR would slice off a piece of the strongest store cheese for each one and pull out the Four Roses bottle he kept in the lima-bean bin. After talking and sipping for a period of time, the politician-hunters often as not decided they needed a Woolrich hunting jacket, or a red wool cap, or gloves, or bullets, or maybe even a 30-06 deer rifle. Or maybe some of each. If they were on a fishing trip, they'd load up on fish hooks, fishing poles, fishing boots, fishing baskets, fishing line, and other fishing stuff LR said they could have at half-price.

One time one of the politician-fishermen who came into the store was none other than the Republican candidate for president running against Mr. Roosevelt. It was in early May of 1935 that the Republican treasurer of Warren County, "Put It Up to Bill," four men dressed in black suits and fedora hats, and Alfred M. Landon, called "the Sunflower Candidate," because he'd been the Governor of Kansas, stopped by to see LR and get their piece of free cheese. They were on their way to a political rally in West Spring Creek where Mr. Landon was going to speak to the farmers about how Roosevelt was neglecting the farmers in the United States, especially the ones in Spring Creek Township.

I happened to be passing through the store to collect a few Ox Heart chocolate drops when Mr. Landon came in. LR told him who I was, and after we'd shaken hands, Mr. Landon hoisted me onto a counter, pinned a big sunflower badge on my shirt and asked if I could read what was on it. I told him it said "Vote for Alfred M. Landon for President!" Then he wanted me to say it again, only this time do it as loud as I could. I shouted at the top of my seven-year-old voice, "Alfred M. Landon for president." And the men in the black suits thought that was pretty funny.

LR gave each one an especially big slab of cheese, telling them what they didn't eat they could use for trout bait. The black suits also thought that was funny, but they weren't Spring Creekers so they didn't know he wasn't just making that up. Older and bigger trout did prefer strong cheese to worms or nightcrawlers, and I guess you couldn't blame them for that. Since Mr. Landon was running for president against Mr. Roosevelt, LR also gave him a big Bowie hunting knife in a decorated leather holster. (The same one I'd had my eye on for a long time.) He told Mr. Landon he'd need it to keep the farmers from beating him up when he told them what a bad president FDR was. ("FDR" stood for Franklin Delano Roosevelt.)

After they left, LR said now that Mr. Landon and I were good friends I could ride over to the rally with him and Uncle Mac. Uncle Mac drove his slaughterhouse truck, and when we went through the gate to Mitchell's pasture where the rally was, a couple of the black suits were passing out Alfred M. Landon badges. It seemed like every farmer in Spring Creek Township was already there with at least one badge hooked onto his overalls. Some of them had probably come to see the next president, but it was more than likely most were there because of the picnic table with big kegs of free beer on it. It was being passed out in red, white and blue cups with "Landon for President" written on one side, and everybody old enough to vote could have as much as they wanted. The farmers' wives and kids got strawberry Kool-Aid out of a big washtub. Our cups were small and white and said "Peters Funeral Home" at the bottom.

Since all the farmers knew LR and Uncle Mac they made way for us to walk right up through the crowd to the stump on which Mr. Landon was going to stand to deliver his speech. Preacher Garner was sitting on it talking to 'PutItUpToBill' and a couple of farmers, but my friend, Mr. Landon, wasn't in sight. LR and Uncle Mac had time to down a couple free cups of beer before 'PutItUpToBill' climbed onto the stump and told everyone to hush. He said he hoped they all liked the beer as much as Preacher Garner did, which made the farmers laugh. Then he told them how Alf was a farmer himself and knew how hard it was for farmers to make a living, especially in these times when someone who doesn't give a damn about farmers is the president. After he'd talked some more about what an honest, hard-working and sincere person Alf Landon was he shouted out, "And now it's time to hear from the next President of the United States, Alfred M. Landon, the Sunflower Candidate from the Great State of Kansas."

Right then a team of horses came through the gate pulling a hay wagon decorated with apple blossoms and American flags. On the wagon were a couple of men in the black suits; Mr. Landon, wearing an Uncle Sam hat; and the three people in the West Spring Creek Grange Square Dance Band. They were playing "Yankee Doodle" on their accordion, fiddle, and saxophone. Mr. Landon was waving both arms at everybody and the black suits were throwing out more sunflower buttons. The farmers all clapped and whistled and waved their cups of beer, and it was tremendously exciting!

When the horses came to a stop, the band quieted down and Preacher Garner climbed onto the stump. He had everyone bow

6

their heads and thank the good Lord for getting Mr. Landon to come all the way to Mitchell's pasture to speak to the good people of Spring Creek Township. Before he said "amen," he mentioned to God that it would be right and fitting for Him to see what He could do about helping the farmers by making sure Mr. Landon won the election next November.

After the preacher had his turn, Mr. Landon jumped down from the wagon onto the stump and told everybody about how with God's help and that of all of the wonderful people right here in Mitchell's pasture, he would be able to replace that devil in Washington who was going to put the US of A right in the poorhouse! He talked for quite awhile about what he'd do once he got to be president, and then, just before he got to the end of what he was going to say, he pointed right at me in the front row and announced there was a young man here from Spring Creek who had something important to tell them.

One of the black suits lifted me up on the stump beside Mr. Landon and whispered in my ear I should hold my badge and yell as loud as I could manage what the badge said. I shouted, "Vote for Alfred M. Landon for President," two times, which got everybody to cheering and clapping their hands. Then Mr. Landon ended his talk by saying it was for all the farmers in Spring Creek Township, and for all the children like John, and that's why it was so important to get Roosevelt out of office next November.

As soon as he'd finished his speech, the West Spring Grange Square Dance Band played (I think it was "The Pennsylvania Polka"), and the farmers clapped and whistled and cheered. Everybody at the rally knew for sure the Devil in Washington had met his match in Mr. Landon. The beer barrels had been drained by that time so the farmers went back to their farms to wait until next November when God and Mr. Landon would chase that slippery-tongued Roosevelt out of the White House.

On election Tuesday that next November, everyone in Spring Creek Township who'd heard Mr. Landon's speech wore their sunflower badges to the Community Building and the other voting places around the township. Most everybody thought for sure they were voting for the next president, Alf. However, unfortunately for Alf, for the Spring Creek Township farmers, and all the children like me, God must have been away from his desk that election day. When the results were announced on the radio the following morning, Mr. Landon had not only lost to Roosevelt, he'd lost by more votes than anybody ever before had lost the presidential election.

But that isn't what happened in Spring Creek Township! When the results were published two days later in the *Warren Times Mirror,* it turned out that in Spring Creek Township Mr. Landon had whipped President Roosevelt by the score of 179 to 57. LR said it must be those fifty-seven people hadn't heard Mr. Landon's and my speech.

# Two

## The Governor Is Rescued
## (By Me and the State Police)

Not all of the distinguished Republican politicians who came up
from Harrisburg to Warren County during the 1930's to hunt
deer or to fish for trout stayed at the Youngsville Hotel, the
Garland Inn, or the Allegheny Hotel in Warren. There was a
small gang of especially distinguished ones who always went
to the Henry farm, two miles east of Spring Creek across the
Brokenstraw Creek from the dirt road to Garland. Before it became the Henry farm it had been the Jackson farm, and that's
where Bob Jackson was born! Some of the politicians were well
acquainted with Bob even though he was an important Democrat, which is how they got to know about the Henry farm.

In case you don't know, Bob Jackson was the same Robert
H. Jackson, who in 1940 became the Attorney General of the
U.S.A., reporting directly to Franklin Delano Roosevelt himself.
After a couple of years Roosevelt nominated him for a job as a
Supreme Court Justice, and Justices don't report to anybody.
Then when World War II ended, it was Robert H. Jackson who
was chief prosecutor at the Nuremberg trials of Nazi war crimi-
nals. All of which made him a pretty important man in Spring
Creek. However, at the time of this story, around 1935, he was
only the Assistant Attorney General.

By the way, Bob's aunt, Miss Jackson, was my Sunday
School teacher and also ran the ice cream parlor when it was in
the lower corner of the store. Bob, himself, had taught her to
put a scoop of vanilla ice cream into a glass of Hire's root beer
and call it a root beer float. It cost a nickel and was very popular
in Spring Creek. Not very often, but once in awhile, her Democrat nephew came to town to see how she was doing. Bob claimed

9

whenever he crossed over the line into Spring Creek Township he automatically turned into a Republican. LR said he was full of crap up to his ears even if he was born in Spring Creek.

The Henry farmhouse was a large, old wooden building with a moss-covered blue-green roof. Once it had been white, but the paint had weathered into several shades of gray. Like most farmhouses in northwest Pennsylvania during the early 1930's, it was without electricity, therefore smoky kerosene lanterns and candles were used for light. During the cold season, which around Spring Creek included spring, summer and fall, the only warm rooms were the kitchen with its wood-burning pot-bellied stove, and the parlor where there was a large fireplace. Water came from a pitcher pump in the kitchen and when you had to go, you went out to the backhouse about half way up the lane to the barn. It was a custom-built three-holer making it plenty big enough, but like the house, it was inclined to be cold and drafty during the winter, wet when it rained, and steaming hot during the summer.

It seemed peculiar to some Spring Creekers that important politicians would want to stay in such a place when everyone knew they could well afford rooms at the Allegheny Hotel in Warren where there were bathrooms right in some of the bedrooms. There were at least three very good reasons why they did: (1) they didn't have to go far from the back door to shoot a deer or two. Deer were regular visitors to a place not far behind Mr. Henry's barn where Mr. Henry put out hay and grain for the deer to eat; (2) to get to the best trout fishing hole between Spring Creek and Garland all they had to do was walk down to Mr. Henry's bridge over the Brokenstraw and drop in a line. In the spring Mr. Henry threw corn, bread crumbs, and dried cheese off the bridge every day, so that area was a hangout for lots of fat trout; and (3) Clifford.

Clifford was a Spring Creeker who had served in World War I in France as a cook for one of the army generals on our side. When the war ended Clifford came home while the general was put in charge of the Pennsylvania National Guard. Clifford was in the National Guard Reserves so he still had to cook for the General every summer when the Guard practiced war down at Indiantown Gap, not far from Harrisburg. The general was one of the especially important politicians who stayed at the Henry farm and he would draft Clifford to be their cook.

Clifford could make venison taste like a T-bone steak. Deer meat, unless it's cooked a special way, tastes pretty much like medium-rare woodchuck and especially important politicians would rather eat T-bones. When it came to cooking trout, everybody said the Waldorf-Astoria in New York City didn't serve up better pan-fried trout then Clifford. More than likely the chefs at the Waldorf didn't know about soaking trout in whisky for an hour before it went into the pan. Or that once it got in the pan it only stayed there while Clifford counted to six.

Clifford bought all the politicians' groceries at LR's general store, and, with LR's help, he made sure the politicians got nothing but the best even if it did cost the most. Then he would use the Spring Creek Township dump truck to take the groceries to the farm. Clifford's job was taking care of the township's dirt roads, so he could drive the truck whenever he wanted, as long as it was on official business. Feeding distinguished politicians was certainly that.

Sometimes after the store closed for the day, LR went to the Henrys' to play poker with the politicians. The deer hunting season just after the election when Mr. Landon was so badly trounced by Roosevelt about every place in the U.S.A. except Spring Creek Township, was the time when LR took me along. This was so he could brag about how it was my political speech that had got all but fifty-seven people in the township to vote Republican. Grandpa Charley had taught me at a young age to play "real" poker, which he had learned from Buffalo Bill Cody back when the Codys lived next door to Grampa Charley's house in St. Joe, Missouri. Because of this, I watched with interest as the general, the governor, two state senators, the state treasurer, and LR competed at five-card-stud and jacks-or-better draw.

All of the poker players were averaging about a shot-and-a-beer per hand played, which meant having to make regular passes to the three-holer out back. The second time LR made the trip he asked the players if I could sit in for him, and they were surprised that such a little boy would know about playing

11

poker. Nobody minded, probably since I was such a good vote-getter, and the governor said, "Welcome aboard, and ante up, sonny." He was probably thinking it would be a good chance to get some more of LR's money.

Clifford brought a pillow for me to sit on in order to see over the edge of the table. I'd already observed that while the governor, the general, the state senators, and the state treasurer all considered themselves serious poker players, they weren't "real" poker players. Real poker players win more money be-cause of how they bet than they do so by what cards they hold.

The first hand of jacks-or-better I won because I was lucky and drew an ace to fill an ace-high straight. The second hand I won by playing "real" poker, bluffing both the governor and the state treasurer into believing I had a pat hand by drawing no cards, then raising twice. When LR returned, the general, who'd lost the most, told him it was a good thing LR hadn't fallen in since they couldn't afford to play with a card shark like me. On the way home I told LR about how I'd won one of the hands with just a pair of threes by drawing no cards and betting "like I really had 'em," as Grampa Charley had taught. LR said that only proved you didn't have to be smart to be a politician.

It was the following spring during trout season when the Pennsylvania state police and I were called upon to rescue the same governor and general, plus three congressmen from the middle of Greeley Run. This was the time the Henry Farm gang decided to give their wives a treat and bring them along to Spring Creek, so they stayed up at the Corry Hotel instead of the Henry Farm. The Governor's wife had said she'd be damned if she and the other women would ride all the way across Penn-sylvania to go to a place where you had to get water from a pump and freeze their asses in an outhouse.

The men fished for three days while the women saw the sights of Corry. That only took about an hour one morning; I don't know just what they did the rest of the time. Then, the Saturday night before the group headed back to the capital on Sunday, the politicians held an important political meeting and fish fry over on the banks of the Spring Creek (creek). LR, being an important Spring Creek Township Republican, was told he was expected to be there, so Ma invited the wives to our house for supper and bridge. Hasty, the whiskey salesman from Corry, who was married to LR's first cousin, was an officer in the National Guard Reserves so he also went to the meeting. Clifford used the Township truck to officially take over the stuff for the important meeting: the beer, whiskey, tables, folding chairs, playing cards, oil lanterns, tubs of ice, a charcoal grill, T-bone steaks and such.

At six o'clock the politicians' two big black Buicks parked in front of our house to let the ladies out and pick up LR. I overheard the Governor's wife tell the general they'd all damn well better be back before eleven to pick them up since they had to get up early the next morning to make that damnable God-awful drive back to Harrisburg.

To get to the important meeting place, the general and Hasty, who were the drivers of the Buicks, had to turn from the West Spring Creek road onto the Jackson Hill road, go a half mile down that, then turn onto a narrow, overgrown cart trail which ran along the bank above the Spring Creek. After two miles of brushing through the trees, the cart path went through the wide, rock-bottomed and hub-cap-deep Greeley Run, near where it flowed into the Spring Creek. On the other side of the ford was a clearing in the woods where the important political meeting and fish fry was held.

Driving through Greeley was a little tricky, but anybody could do it if they went slow enough so as not to drown the motor, yet fast enough to not lose traction on the slippery rocks. If a car stopped it sometimes was very difficult to get it moving again. As I said, anybody could do it, so the general and Hasty both made it across with no trouble.

Ma's dinner went well even though my two older sisters, M. and H., were waitresses. Aunt Martha, from next door and Mrs. Maxwell, from up back, did the cooking, and Grampa Charley and I washed the dishes. Doing the dishes took a long time because the ladies had a different plate for everything they ate. On top of that, Ma used her best company china and the rule was that we'd better not break even one piece. When we'd finished it was after nine o'clock so Ma sent us directly upstairs to bed. The ladies said good night and how cute we were, and I thought that's the last I'd be seeing of them.

The next morning Ma woke me up just when it was beginning to get light. She asked if I knew just where the men had gone to have their meeting, and of course I did, since where the Greeley poured into the Spring Creek was about the best brook trout fishing spot in the county. She said the men had never come back from the meeting and all the women were worried sick about what might have happened. She and the governor's wife were going down to the store to call the state police (we didn't have a phone at the house), and I was to show them how to get to the meeting place. When I got downstairs all the ladies were standing by the large front window watching the corner down by the store since that's where they'd first see the Buicks if the men ever made it back.

Ma unlocked the store and she and the governor's wife hustled to the phone which was on the wall behind the cash register. It took several cranks on the phone to wake up Mrs. Brown, the operator. Then, when Ma told Mrs. Brown she wanted to call the state police in Corry, Mrs. Brown wanted to know whatever for. Ma said she didn't have time to say, and she knew Mrs. Brown would find out soon enough by listening in, which she always did.

One of the police answered the phone, and Ma told him about the missing men. She listened for a minute then turned from the phone to tell the governor's wife he'd said he was sorry but since Spring Creek was in Warren County she would have to call the state police down in Warren. (Corry, in Erie County, was six miles away; Warren was twenty-one). The governor's wife said, "Give me that goddamn phone!" I don't suppose she knew that Ma was a church deacon. Then the governor's wife took a deep breath and shouted, "It's the Governor of the state who's missing and I'm the governor's wife and you're going to be a god-damned lot sorrier if you don't get off your fat asses and get down to Spring Creek right now."

That must have made Mrs. Branch sit up and take notice. It certainly worked for the Corry state police because in about ten minutes two state police cars with their sirens going and red bubble lights flashing arrived in Spring Creek in a cloud of dust.

14

All four of the state police assigned to the Corry barracks hurried through the store's front door. Ma started telling them about the important political meeting but the governor's wife interrupted, saying they'd better find the governor pretty damned fast, or else—like it was their fault he hadn't come home all night. Ma managed to finish her story, then she told them I would show them where to look. I rode in the first police car with Corporal Bruce who was the one in charge. He turned on the siren even though there wasn't another car on the road, and in less than five minutes we got to the Jackson Hill road turnoff. The only house between the turnoff and the creek was old Mr. Boils's place, and there on the front porch were the governor, LR and old Mr. Boils holding a shotgun. I pointed them out to Bruce and the two police cars skidded to a stop in front of the house.

The police jumped out of the cars and pulled out their pistols, yelling for old Mr. Boils to drop the gun. The governor waved at them and hollered for the police not to worry; Mr. Boils wasn't going to shoot anybody. Then the governor asked the police if they might be looking for him and Corporal Bruce said they'd been told by his wife to find him, by God, or else. Everybody chuckled about that except the governor. Then LR and the governor got into Corporal Bruce's car where I was, and we headed for the old cart path. On the way to the Greeley Run, LR and the governor told the policemen what had happened.

After the important political meeting was over about eleven o'clock, they'd climbed into the Buicks to drive back to Spring Creek. This time the governor drove the first car because the general seemed to be very tired. The trouble was, nobody had advised the governor to go slow and steady through the Greeley, so he went fast and jerky, and halfway across the motor got wet and died. The second car, driven by Hasty, had to stop because the general's car was in the way. Once he stopped, Hasty couldn't go forward because of car number one, and couldn't back up because of the slippery rocks.

Nobody worried much right then because Clifford would soon be coming in the Township dump truck and he'd be able to pull the cars out. However, when Clifford arrived fifteen minutes later there were two problems: he couldn't get the truck past

15

the two cars because of the big rocks in the creek on either side of the ford; and he didn't have the township tow rope with him anyway. Clifford tried pushing the two big Buicks in front of the township truck, but their weight and the slippery bottom made the going difficult and slow. After an hour some progress had been made but then the township dump truck ran out of gas.

Another important political meeting to decide what to do was held then and there in the middle of the Greeley. The politicians voted that at first light, LR who knew the way, and the governor, who was responsible for their being stuck there, would go out to the road and get gasoline from somebody for the Township truck.

Old Mrs. Boils's house was the first house they came to, so that's why they were on the porch. LR told the policeman when he and the governor went up and knocked on the door, old Mr. Boils had shouted from inside for them to go away. The governor yelled back that he was the governor of Pennsylvania and he needed some gasoline. Old Mr. Boils figuring they were hoboes or gypsies, shouted that if he didn't get his Governor's ass offen his front porch, he'd help him get it off with a load of buckshot. Then LR told old Mr. Boils who he was, and, recognizing LR's voice, old Mr. Boils opened the door. It was just then when the police had shown up.

When we drove up to the Greeley ford the governor told Corporal Bruce to turn on the siren. Then he was to shout that they were under arrest for parking in the Greeley Run. The men from the important meeting were sleeping in the cars and Clifford was asleep in the truck, but the noise and shouting woke up everybody in a hurry.

One of the policemen waded out and tried starting the first car. The motor must have dried out by then since it took right off, and he drove it the rest of the way through the Greeley. Another policeman drove Hasty's Buick across, after which the police gave Clifford a five-gallon can of emergency gas to put into the Township dump truck. Soon the two police cars, followed by the two Buicks followed by the Township dump truck, were on their way back to Spring Creek.

When the procession pulled up in front of our house, the governor's wife led the wives as they marched down to the street.

16

They all appeared quite angry instead of being happy that their menfolk had been rescued, and the governor's wife was the angriest of all. She told the governor in front of everybody that he looked like a drunken bum and asked just where the Hell he'd been all night. The other ladies started fussing much the same way. Then Corporal Bruce of the state police stepped between the governor and his wife and informed her, loud enough for everybody to hear, about how the men had worked hard most of the night trying to get the cars from where they were trapped in the middle of Greeley Run. He also told how the governor and LR had walked all the way out of the woods for help, and how the governor had almost been shot.

His speech got the governor's wife and the other ladies to simmer down and begin feeling a bit sorry for what the men had gone through. I was surprised a state police corporal would tell such a big lie. Then Bruce said everybody should get in their cars and be escorted back to the Corry Hotel before the hotel people began wondering if something bad had happened to their distinguished guests.

The ladies must have liked Ma's dinner because a few days later she got thank-you letters from everybody except the governor's wife. I suppose that was because the governor's wife seemed to think LR and Clifford were to blame for everything, even though it was the governor who had got everybody stuck in the Greeley. The governor must have liked what Corporal Bruce had said to his wife because two weeks later Sergeant Bruce stopped by the store for his free piece of store cheese.

# Three
## LR's Doggone Joke

I said before that during the 1930's Spring Creek was a busy town even if it wasn't very big. Still, since the 1930's was when Mr. Hoover's Great Depression was in full bloom, quite a few Spring Creek men weren't able to get jobs, even in President Roosevelt's WPA. To pass the time, some of these men stopped by the post office in the store several times a day to check out their mail. They did this although they knew as well as anybody that a mailbag was tossed off the *Pennsylvania Flier* just twice a day, at 7:00 A.M. and 7:00 P.M. After examining their empty mail boxes, as often as not they'd spend the next hour or so loafing in the store, particularly in winter since the store with its oil furnace and steam radiators was warmer than most houses with their wood-burning Franklin stoves.

One of the store's six radiators was beneath the counter in the dry goods section where ladies' dresses, men's shirts and overalls, ladies' and men's underwear, stockings, shoes and such as that were kept. The wooden counter-top was always comfortably warm, consequently it was the favorite place for loafers to—in Aunt Hat's words—"plant their fat asses." Not only would their fat hindquarters be warmed, but they could also sometimes observe whose womenfolk were buying what kind of underwear.

To be sure, neither LR nor Uncle Glen approved of the loafers sitting there, nevertheless they didn't mention it, being afraid that the loafers might get upset and not pay their grocery bills. Which most of them usually couldn't pay anyway. Eventually LR, who, like Uncle Mac, was a pretty good practical joker, invented a way to get them to remove their fat behinds off the counter without having to be told. All it took was a long piece of twine, an eight-penny nail sharpened with a file, and a few boards. From the far end of the counter where he couldn't be seen, LR jerked the string and the nail popped up through a crack in the counter top, jabbing the sitter clean through his overalls and long johns. Then the nail dropped back down out of sight, so when the loafer rolled his rump to find out what had stabbed him there'd be nothing to see. After a couple jabs, in some particularly hard cases, three, the loafer would stand up and walk away looking like he was worrying about his coming down with the rheumatism.

Then there was another time when one of LR's practical jokes ended a bothersome situation with a bank president from the city of Corry. It took place during deer-hunting season when men (and even a few women) came from all over to hunt in the hills around Spring Creek, since there were so many deer you had to be a pretty bad shot not to get one. A few local hunters who were regular store customers sometimes brought some of their deer meat to the store for LR to grind into deerburger and wrap up in one- or two-pound packages. They either paid to have it done or gave LR a package or two of the burger since LR never had the time to go out and shoot his own deer. The bank president, who most Spring Creek Township farmers referred to as that damned skinflint, also brought his deer meat in for grinding. However, being a damned skinflint, he never once offered to pay LR a penny, nor did he ever present him with as much as a pound of deerburger. To make matters worse, the bank president wasn't a store customer, and in fact never spent a nickel there saying he could get everything a lot cheaper up in Corry.

LR, being a good businessman, wasn't about to get on the wrong side of a bank president, so for several years he ground and packaged the bank president's deerburger free of charge. Then came the year when the bank president complained that LR was taking too long to get the job done, and it was the next hunting season LR played the practical joke which got the bank president to take his grinding business elsewhere.

One freezing cold morning a few days before December 1st, the first day of deer season, LR discovered a deceased and frozen Andy Gump lying next to the store's burn pile behind the store. Andy Gump, in case you never heard of him, was a fat old tramp

19

dog that toured Spring Creek every morning begging scraps at people's back doors. He ended up each day at the burn pile behind the store expecting a dinner of discarded baloney, spoiled wieners or moldy liver and usually spent the night near the rear cellar door where some heat escaped through the bottom crack. Since Andy Gump was old and fat, LR wasn't surprised that he'd passed on, and seeing him lying there LR got the idea for the practical joke. Andy Gump's fat behind reminded him of the bank president.

LR put Andy into a burlap bag and stowed him in an old refrigerator in the back room of the store. Deer season arrived, and sure enough, a few days later the bank president waddled into the store carrying a box of deer chunks for grinding. As soon as he saw him coming through the front door, LR hurried to the back room, took Andy Gump out of the refrigerator, pulled him from the bag and hung him on a hook near the meat grinder. Then he went back out and told the bank president it was OK for him to carry his meat out to the grinding table.

When he plopped his venison on the grinding table the bank president saw Andy Gump. He asked LR just what the hell was that dog doing there, and LR replied there were quite a few farmers around who regularly brought in raccoons, groundhogs, and sometimes even dead dogs to be ground up. The bank president said you don't mean in *this* grinder? and LR said yes, since that's the only grinder he had. Right then without another word the bank president scooped up his deer meat, carried it back out to his Cadillac and headed back to Corry. He never came back into the store again, even though not just a few people made a special point of telling the damned skinflint that LR had only been playing a doggoned joke on him!

# Four
## The Night the Devil Came
## to Play Bridge

Hasty, short for Hastings, was a professional basketball player (Pennsylvania Keystones), a professional hockey player (I don't know what team), and a professional golfer. During the 1930s, professional athletes didn't get paid much so they sold life insurance or whiskey. Hasty was very well known around Corry and Spring Creek because he was the six-foot-four whiskey salesman.

I mentioned in a previous chapter he was married to LR's cousin Esther, and they lived in a not very big apartment in Corry since Hasty wasn't home much. When they wanted to have a party, which they did quite often, it had to be at somebody's house where there'd be room for everybody. That's why one Saturday night in late July, Esther had a going-away party for Hasty at our house in Spring Creek. For the next two weeks he would be practicing war with the Pennsylvania National Guard at Indiantown Gap.

The men were playing poker at the kitchen table, drinking beer and bourbon courtesy of Hasty, the whiskey salesman; the ladies were playing bridge in the living room, drinking tea courtesy of Ma, the church deacon. Certain of the ladies, namely Aunt Ha, Miss Allen and Miss Harris (teachers at the Spring Creek Grade school), and Aunt Esther, also made regular trips to the kitchen to "check on the poker game," and spike their tea with bourbon.

Aunt Mildred, LR's sister, was at the party, but Uncle Mac had to make a special trip over to Spartensburg to pick up some animals for the slaughterhouse, so he wasn't going to be there

22

until later. About three-quarters through the first bottle of bourbon something made a loud thump on the back porch. Clifford, the National Guard cook for General Hershey, said, "I'll bet that there's old Mac now."

I was in the kitchen watching the poker game, and LR told me to open the door to let old Mac in, but he wasn't there. Nobody was. A few minutes later there was another loud thump and the doorknob rattled as though someone had their hand on it. This time when I opened the door someone, or rather, *something*, was certainly there. Something which smelled awful and was taller than the door itself when it reared up on its hind legs. Something which caused a certain six-going-on-seven-year-old kid to very nearly wet his pants.

Leaving the door wide open, I scampered to the far side of the table so it and the men would be between me and whatever it was. Through the door clomped a huge, gray, smelly, long-horned billy goat dragging behind him the rope tied around his neck. The poker players jumped to their feet, tipping over some chairs, beer bottles and a glass or two. Hasty said, "What in damnation?" and George, the boss at the milk plant, threw his bottle of beer at it. None of this was appreciated by the goat so he trotted right through the kitchen and into the hallway leading to the living room where the ladies were.

The ladies had of course heard the noise and cussing going on in the kitchen so Aunt Hat was on her way up that same hallway to see what was going on. When she saw the silhouette of the big horned goat coming toward her, she, being an Irish Catholic, thought, "The Devil himself had come to play bridge!" She let out a screech that threw a terrible scare into the ladies back in the living room, as well as the goat. He bolted past Aunt Hat, who was frozen stiff, and skidded into the living room. Now it was the ladies' turn to jump and yell. One of the card tables was upset, and tea, cups, saucers, cards and cookies went all over the floor. Again the goat didn't much like all the hullabaloo so he made for higher ground, heading out of the living room into the front hall and up the stairs.

Upstairs in his room Grampa Charley also had heard the commotion, even though his ears weren't too good. He had just started down the steps to investigate when he met the goat head on. Unlike Aunt Hat, Grampa Charley knew the difference between a goat and the Devil, so he whacked it on its head with his cane which made the goat change his mind about climbing up any further.

Most of the men and ladies had gathered in the front hall near the bottom of the stairway. When the goat headed back down in their direction, their ladies scurried back into the living room, while LR swung open the front door, expecting the goat would make a dash for freedom. The goat apparently wasn't quite ready to leave the party yet, and, rather than heading out the door, he trotted toward the dining room on the other side of the front hall from the living room.

In the dining room was the round glass china closet where Ma stored all of her best dishes, glasses, and stuff like that. Since the goat was heading in that direction, Ma took immediate defensive action. Grabbing the legs of the overturned card table, she charged after the goat into the dining room, and holding the table like a shield, got between it and the china closet. This was a good maneuver, but it forced the goat to get close to the dining room table which had been set up with a lace table cloth, coffee cups, saucers, and plates. One of the goat's long horns hooked into the table cloth, pulling it and all the dishes onto the floor. The crash was so loud the goat finally became convinced he didn't want to stay in this noisy house a minute longer.

Between the dining room and the kitchen was a swinging door, and somehow the goat knew it was the best way out. Butting it open with his head, he was back in familiar territory with nothing between him and the wide open back door but scattered beer bottles, chairs, glasses, and the tipped-over chairs. The goat trotted directly for the door but Ma wasn't about to let him get away with the lace table cloth which was still hooked on his horn. She grabbed the rope dragging behind him, which slowed him just enough for Clifford to catch up and get hold of the rope himself. Clifford was the only man at the party in the same weight class as the goat, therefore he was able to stop him long enough for Ma to unhook the cloth. Then Clifford followed the goat out the door and tied him to a column on the back porch. He said he'd take the goat to his house later when he went home; however, by that time the goat had mysteriously disappeared.

With all the folks pitching in, cleaning up the mess they and the goat had made didn't take long. A few cups and dishes were demolished, but the lace tablecloth wasn't hurt a bit. On the other hand, the old billy-goat smell was still thick in every room of the house, and any farmer will tell you an old goat smells worse than a bag of rotten potatoes. Everyone was sure Uncle Mac was behind all this because who else would possibly have had a goat to let into the house. Yet across the street at Uncle Mac's house there were no lights on, and his old Chevy truck wasn't parked outside in the driveway. Maybe it wasn't Uncle Mac after all who'd played such a stinking trick!

Well, to make a long story a bit shorter, it turned out the old goat had been one of Uncle Mac's riders back from Spartensburg. After stopping for a "few-for-the-road" at the Route 77 Tavern on the way home, Uncle Mac concluded it would be a good trick on the poker players to tie the big, smelly goat to our back door. He drove his truck around behind Aunt Martha's barn in back of our house, walked the goat to the door and looped the rope around the knob. What he hadn't counted on was the loop slipping off when the door was opened. Peeking around the corner of the barn, Uncle Mac watched the goat invite himself to the party, then heard all the turmoil and excitement. He knew he'd be blamed, and since he was already a bit afraid of Ma, knowing just how provoked she could get at certain times, Uncle Mac decided he'd better try covering his tracks.

He stood watch from behind the barn expecting that sooner or later the goat would come out the same way it went in. His idea was to catch and hide it some good place so nobody could prove he knew anything about it. After Clifford tied the goat on the back porch and went back in the house, Uncle Mac hurried down, untied the rope and led the goat away, leaving his truck where he'd concealed it behind the barn.

Uncle Mac might have gotten away with it except for one thing; goats don't care what they eat. The goat-hiding place Uncle Mac had picked was his old office in the abandoned cold storage building next door to his house. The office was at the front of the building facing the road, but nobody would see the goat because of the big, old heavy-duty roll-down green shade that had covered the large window for the last thirty years.

By the time it was light the next morning, the goat had eaten most of the shade and, just as Aunt Hat was driving by on her way to early Mass at St. Joseph's up in Corry, he was standing on his back legs in front of the window trying to reach the leftovers. Aunt Hat knew that right there in Uncle Mac's old office was the Devil Who'd Come to Play Bridge!

# Five
## Turkeys Talk, You Know

The slaughterhouse, which Uncle Mac owned, was where chickens and turkeys lost their heads and feathers, and pigs, cows, sheep, goats, and calves were turned into roasts, chops, steaks, beef hearts and tongues, and such as that. Sometimes, before I was old enough to be in school, Uncle Mac would take me with him when he drove his old red Chevy truck to collect the animals. It was on one of these trips that a big tom turkey talked to me.

Uncle Mac parked the truck beside Farmer Watauski's barn and we walked up a dirt lane toward the house to let him know we'd arrived. On either side of the lane and in the back yard were chickens, geese, and turkeys, and one of the turkeys, the one almost as tall as I was, followed us right up onto the back porch. Before Uncle Mac had a chance to knock, the turkey tapped loudly on the door with his beak and began to gobble.

When the farmer came out of the house he patted the turkey's back as if it were a dog. Uncle Mac told him I was LR's boy, and Farmer Watauski said the only boy he had was that turkey, Frank. Frank had been named after President Roosevelt.

Uncle Mac, the farmer, Frank and I walked side by side toward the barn. We'd gone only a short ways when the turkey said in a plain but squawky voice, "How come you're not in school today?" I'd never been close to a big live turkey before so I decided it must be they can talk. Ma's friend, Mrs. Jessup, had a talking parrot, although mostly it just swore at people, so why couldn't turkeys? I told Frank it was because I wasn't big enough, and then the turkey said, "You sure look big enough to me!" By then we'd reached the barn and Farmer Watauski shooed Frank back towards the farmhouse.

On the way back to the slaughterhouse with the calf in a wooden crate in the back of the truck, I told Uncle Mac I didn't know that turkeys could talk. He said not many people did because they were very particular about who they would talk to. Then he said they also prayed, especially around Thanksgiving time. Which was only a few weeks away.

Thanksgiving Day at our house was a big family-and-relatives affair. Aunt Martha always brought corn bread and pumpkin pies; Aunt Hat, who wasn't a very good cook, brought her green Jell-O and carrot salad; Aunt Mildred the sweet potatoes and raisin pies; and Aunt Mary her creamed stringbean, mushroom and walnut casserole. Grampa Charley made the mashed potatoes and Ma did the turkey, stuffing it, cooking it overnight, and making the gravy.

When we were all seated at the table and Uncle Lon was saying grace it occurred to me we were going to be eating something that talked and prayed. Providing it hadn't been cooked overnight, of course. Right after Uncle Lon finished being thankful and before anybody said anything, I announced, "Turkeys talk, you know! And they pray a lot at Thanksgiving time!"

Everybody began laughing, even Uncle Glen, who seldom laughed much at anything. (LR said he'd be the same way if he had to live with Aunt Hat.) Aunt Hat, who was a Catholic and had sneaked a bite of roll during grace, laughed so hard she blew it out all over her end of the table. When it got quiet again, Ma asked what in the world made me think turkeys talked and prayed. I told about how Uncle Mac and I had talked to one at the Watauski farm, and that Uncle Mac had told me about how they prayed at Thanksgiving.

Aunt Hat shrieked, "I knew it; I knew Mac had something to do with this." Then Uncle Mac said I was absolutely right; turkeys could talk, but they only talked to little folks and Democrats. Maybe you never knew Uncle Mac was a Democrat, but he was. In fact LR regularly reminded him he was the "only damned Democrat in the whole damned family." Which, of course, explains why he and I were the only ones at that dinner who knew turkeys talked.

# Six
## The Great Garbage Ambush

If Spring Creek would have had a pool hall for certain big boys, namely, Hacker, Baldy, Weiner, Jules and Ern, to hang around in, the Great Garbage Ambush probably would not have occurred. Having nothing much better to do, they often passed the time by playing games with certain of us little guys, namely Tuffy, Jinx, George, Roo, Teddy, and me. As far as we were concerned, the games were not much fun. Dutch-rub, for instance, was played by pinning our little arms to the ground with their hard knobby knees, and rubbing our little heads with their hard grubby knuckles. When one of them held our arms behind our backs and another flicked at our noses with their long, strong dirty fingers, that was Snap-nose. Heave-ho, their favorite game, was played down by the railroad depot where the ground was covered with cinders. Two of the older boys swung one of us back and forth by our hands and feet finally letting go, heaving us as far as they could.

In the winter we were targets for the big boys' snowballs; in the spring it was mudballs; and in summer their ammunition was green apples. Inasmuch as they could all throw much harder and further than any of us, our one defense was to scurry about like cornered mice and at the first opportunity try to run away. Unfortunately, they could also run faster.

Most grownups in Spring Creek believed Hacker, Baldy, Weiner, Jules and Ern, were nice boys. Hacker, Baldy, and Weiner went to Sunday School, Jules tended the wood burning stoves at the grade school, and Ern made money cutting lawns and shoveling snow for folks who were too old to do it themselves. This was why our Ma's and Pa's paid no attention when we tattled about the way we were being mistreated, so the big boys' games continued for at least a couple years. It was only after the Great Garbage Ambush down at the garbage building that they left us alone.

The roofless concrete shell of one of the old tannery buildings was where many Spring Creekers dumped their garbage. The garbage building, as it was called, was built into the side of a high bank next to the railroad tracks. The top of one side of the building was level with the railroad bed, while the opposite wall stood over two stories high. At the bottom of that wall were two doorways about twenty feet apart. Each had a wooden door which always hung open but could be swung shut on its rusty hinges. Garbage was dumped over the wall next to the tracks, and at the time of the ambush the back side of the building was almost half full of bottles, cans, paper, corn cobs, foul-smelling globs of rotting meat and vegetables, and such as that. Plus lots of rats!

One of my Sunday chores, for which I was paid a paltry allowance of forty cents, was to haul our garbage cans down to the garbage building in my red wagon. This was hard work, especially when it came to carrying the heavy cans over the ungraded railroad tracks and dumping the contents over the edge of the building. That's why I paid Tuffy, Jinx, and George each a nickel to help. Since they got no allowance, they were ready and waiting most Saturday mornings.

One day the four of us were about to carry the cans over the tracks when we heard voices inside the building. I cautiously peeked over the edge and down there shooting BB guns at the rats were the two older boys we feared the most, Hacker and Wiener. This would definitely not be a good time to dump the cans, so I retreated back across the tracks and whispered to the others we'd better come back later in the day.

Jinx didn't agree. What he wanted for us to do was sneak down the bank to the lower side of the building, then quickly close the two doors and prop them shut. By trapping Hacker and Wiener inside, we could throw garbage down at them until it was all gone and have plenty of time to run away. The idea was scary and stupid as far as I was concerned, but Tuffy and George immediately sided with Jinx, so we began phase one of the garbage ambush.

George and I crept down the steep bank at the left side of the building; Jinx and Tuffy went down on the right. At the bottom, each team carefully approached the nearest doorway carrying along a couple of the old boards that were strewn about the tannery grounds. At Jinx's signal we simultaneously swung the doors shut, propped them firmly in place with the boards, then scrambled back up the bank. From up above we watched Hacker and Wiener try to push the door open, shouting bad swear words and saying whoever was out there had better open the doors or else. Much to my great surprise and relief, the scheme had actually worked. No matter how hard they butted against them, neither door budged an inch.

While Hacker and Weiner continued shoving on the doors we lugged our garbage pails over to the edge of the building. Empty cans, old magazines, soggy newspaper-wrapped bundles of garbage, a pair of Grampa Charley's old shoes, and apple cores rained down on the two of them and now it was their turn to run about like cornered mice. They shouted even worse swear words and began shooting BB's at us. At that distance BB's don't hurt much, but we had to watch we didn't get shot in the eye. This threw our aim off a bit; however, we still scored some good hits, particularly with the rotting potatoes we'd saved until last.

Our last potato had just been hurled when we saw Jules riding up the old tannery road on his bicycle. (Jules made regular trips to the garbage building to see if there was anything he could use.) We panicked, knowing Hawker and Weiner would be free within minutes and we'd never seen them in a worse mood. The four of us dashed across the tracks toward the road, leaving the garbage pails behind, but I grabbed my wagon, knowing I'd never see it again in one piece if I left it behind.

By the time we'd run up the road as far as the old cold storage building, the three big boys were up on the road and gaining fast. Unless we disappeared completely, we were in serious trouble, and the only place in which to disappear was the forbidden cold storage building itself. That was one place they wouldn't look for us because Uncle Mac had PRIVATE PROPERTY—KEEP OUT—THIS MEANS YOU signs on the building's four locked and barred doors.

Despite his signs and our Ma's orders to "stay out of there

because it's likely to fall down any moment," we had been using it as a meeting place and hideout for quite some time. Getting in was no problem if you knew about the small basement window at the rear of the building. It couldn't be seen from the street, the store, or Uncle Mac's house, and was hardly noticeable even when you stood beside it. The latch had rusted away so a push was all that was required to swing the window open. Entering feet first, you dropped onto piles of moldy old sheep hides, and slid to the floor. To get out, the procedure was reversed. The basement was damp, dark and smelled of those moldy sheep skins so we climbed the rickety stairs on the other side of the basement to the third floor where there were four large cork-lined rooms.

Two rooms were located on each side of the building, separated by a hallway at the end of which was an elevator shaft. The elevator, once raised and lowered by ropes and pulleys, was open on both sides and had been left suspended between two of the third floor rooms when the building was abandoned. It was in one of those two rooms that we holed up, since from there we had a good chance to escape should anyone come looking for us. Our reasoning was this: Anybody climbing the creaky stairs would be heard, no matter how hard they tried to be silent. As soon as we knew they had entered the room at the top of the stairs, our plan called for us to run across the elevator into the room on the other side. Then we were to run through the door into the fourth room and out the second door which led to the landing at the top of the stairs. Then it was down the stairs to the basement and back out the window.

Huddled in room three, panting from our run from the garbage building and the hurried climb up the three flights of stairs, we believed we were safe. Then, if we could keep out of their clutches for just a few more days, maybe they wouldn't be quite so mad anymore and wouldn't hurt us too much. We didn't really believe the big boys would carry out their threat to kill us all, because murder was something Spring Creekers weren't allowed to do.

On the other hand, we knew we certainly would be made to suffer for ambushing Hawker and Wiener; the question was, to what extent? That was the very question which panicked me from the moment we ran away from the garbage building. Which is why I was in such a hurry to disappear into the cold storage building that I left my wagon right beside the window. I knew we were in serious trouble.

Sure enough, in but a few minutes we heard the steps begin to creak and groan as the big boys started up. After they reached the first floor there were a few minutes of silence while they searched each room. Then more creaks and groans as they climbed the next flight of stairs, followed by another period of quiet while they checked out the second floor. Now we heard them start up the last flight of steps, and, thinking for sure they had us cornered, the big boys began to yell terrible, nerve-shattering threats about what was to become of us.

For us to escape successfully, patience and good timing were critical. The second we knew Hawker, Wiener, and Jules had entered the first room, we dashed through the elevator into the opposite room. Then it was into and through the final room to the stairway, but just when we reached it we heard a loud, sharp noise, immediately followed by a long loud squeal, a rumble, and finally a loud crash which came from way down below, most likely the basement.

For a moment it was very still, then we heard Jules, who somehow had magically beaten us down to the basement, yelled what sounded very much like, "Jesus and God Damn It!" Hawker was there too because we heard him say "sonovabitch," several times. At that instant, Weiner ran by us and bounded down the stairs.

All of this was quite frightening and confusing. Were they setting up some sort of trap for us, or what? For a few minutes we waited at the top of the stairs during which time we began to hear moans and more cuss words down in the basement. If they were planning to trap us, they certainly wouldn't be making such a fuss, so we gingerly descended to the basement. There in the dusty, dim light at the bottom of the elevator shaft, we saw Weiner bending over Hawker and Jules who were sitting on the floor of the same elevator we'd scampered through on the third floor. The old ropes holding it had broken when Hawker and Jules had stomped through at the same time. Weiner, a pace or so behind, had just missed the ride down.

Hawker was clutching his right leg, the one which seemed attached sort of backwards. Jules tried to stand but sat down with a cry of pain. This was very disconcerting, therefore the four of us promptly headed for the back window, crawling out about the same time Uncle Mac went in the front door to see what had caused the loud crash.

A few minutes later from our porch we watched Uncle Mac and Weiner half carry, half drag Hawker and Jules out the front door of the cold storage building, and lift them into the back of Uncle Mac's truck. Weiner got in beside Uncle Mac and they drove off toward Corry where Uncle Mac delivered them to the Corry Hospital. Hawker had a broken leg, Jules two badly sprained knees and a dislocated hip. They might have been really hurt if not for the thick layer of cork on the floor of the elevator.

Uncle Mac was very angry that the big boys hadn't heeded his KEEP OUT, THIS MEANS YOU signs, and he let them know about it while they were getting patched up at the hospital. When the news got around Spring Creek about them having trespassed, quite a few people around Spring Creek decided maybe they weren't such good boys after all. Interestingly, they never told anybody the real reason why they were in the cold storage building, and it wasn't because they didn't want us little guys to get into trouble. The fact of the matter was they didn't want anybody to know how us little guys had outsmarted them.

By the time Hawker and Jules had recovered enough to start playing games with us again, they didn't. Nor did Weiner, Baldy, or Ern. Maybe this was because they'd learned a good lesson about not messing with us. Or maybe it was because they'd gotten old enough to begin running after girls instead of little guys. Of course, us little guys were also getting bigger, too. It might have been better for the next crop of little guys if Spring Creek would have had a pool hall for us to hang around in.

# Seven

## Mrs. McGee

Mrs. McGee lived in the yellow house up on the Blue Eye Hill road halfway between the store and the church. She had been LR's grade teacher which made her pretty old, but it certainly didn't seem like she was. The reason was Mrs. McGee was probably the most talented person in the whole town of Spring Creek. Spring Creek Township, for that matter.

First of all, Mrs. McGee could whistle so well she usually won first prize at the Ladies Aid Society's Annual Talent Show. (Not always, as you will learn in another chapter.) She played the piano, and could thump a tambourine and shake castanets about as good as anybody. Bird calls, which she always did as an encore to her whistling act, was another of her accomplishments. Here she was most likely better than anybody in the whole state, and when Mrs. McGee strutted about the stage flapping her arms and crowing like a rooster, it was the funniest sight you ever saw.

Mrs. McGee was also famous for her sugar-covered doughnuts, molasses cookies, and candied apples which usually were the first things to sell out at bake sales. Every Halloween, trick-or-treaters stopped at her house first to be sure they'd get a big, warm doughnut, a candied Northern Spy apple on a stick, and a glass of cinnamon-spiced warm cider to wash them down. The peculiar thing was no matter what you dressed up as, Mrs. McGee always guessed your name on her first try.

Sometimes Mrs. McGee substituted at the grade school and even the big kids in the seventh and eighth grades were glad when that happened. Mrs. McGee spent a lot of time reading out loud from books she brought from her house, and listening to her was better than listening to the radio. When different people in the book spoke, she'd use different voices so you could tell who was doing the talking. You knew right away whether it was Alice or the Red Queen; Tom Sawyer or Becky Thatcher, Captain Ahab or Captain Bligh, or Peck's Bad Boy and his Pa. Furthermore, she did sound effects; dogs barked, horses whinnied, frogs croaked, trains huffed and whistled, and the Headless Horseman galloped across a wooden bridge. Ma said Mrs. McGee was remarkable because she brought books to life.

Something else Mrs. McGee could do was tell fortunes, which she did every year at the annual Spring Bazaar in the community building. The bazaar was where you could buy homemade fudge, maple sugar candy, all sorts of homemade pies, pillows, rag dolls made from old stockings, hand-made walking canes, aprons, wooden milk stools, knitted hats, pot holders, dried flowers, and things like that. Almost everything was made and donated by Spring Creek area people to raise money to help out folks who were poorer than they were. Quite a few people traveled from Corry, Garland and all around the township to go to the bazaar.

At the bazaar there was a fishing trough where for a nickel you could try to hook little wooden fish as they floated by. The prize you won depended on what number was painted on the bottom of the fish. There was a booth for pitching pennies, one for throwing darts at balloons, and another where for a nickel you tried to knock down wooden milk bottles with a baseball. The prizes weren't worth much more than what you paid, except for the hoop toss. For a penny you could try to toss a little bamboo hoop over a pack of gum, a Mounds or Mars candy bar, a tin whistle, a rubber ball and such as that, all donated by LR and Uncle Glen's store.

The last booth was where Lady Fat-emma told your fortune for a nickel. Lady Fat-emma's fortune telling booth was a sort of tent made out of bed sheets with cardboard stars and moons pinned on them. Outside the tent a lady dressed like a gypsy, most often it was Mrs. Sitler, sold tickets and made everybody stand in line. When it was your turn she'd hold up a corner of the sheet to let you inside where Lady Fat-emma was sitting at a card table with a green cloth on it. She wore a big white turban, a purple robe and a heavy black veil over her face. All you could see was her glasses, and that's how you knew it was Mrs. McGee; her glasses were thick and had black rims. Because the fortune telling tent wasn't very big and since some farmers didn't do a very good job cleaning their boots before they came to the bazaar, Mrs. McGee always kept incense burning in an old brass pot.

Lady Fat-emma would motion for you to sit in the chair across from her, then lay ten playing cards face down on the table. She'd have you point at six of them which she arranged in a triangle while she told you about how each card meant a different thing. The other four cards she put off to the side, still face down. One by one she turned over the cards from the triangle, starting with the money card, the one people were most interested in. After that came the travel card telling if you'd be going someplace or another. The next one was the romance card, which at that time didn't interest me a bit, followed by the prudence card about things you needed to watch out for. I forget what the last two cards were for. When all six cards had been turned over and she'd finished telling your fortune, she'd push the other four cards back in front of you saying these were the good luck cards. The more aces there were, the luckier you were going to be for the rest of your natural life. Then she'd turn them over one by one, and everybody got four aces. Ma said Mrs. McGee did that trick so everybody would believe they got their nickel's worth.

A lot of Fat-emma's fortunes—that is to say, Mrs. McGee's fortunes—came true! Sooner or later. Like the time she told my friend George he'd soon be going on a trip north, and the very next week his family went on the train to visit his grandparents up in Erie. Mrs. McGee told many folks who'd never been further away from Spring Creek than maybe Warren that someday they'd be journeying to far off and exotic places; places they'd never even heard about. And she was certainly right about that! Not many years later the U.S. Government paid the way for quite a few draft age Spring Creekers to visit places like England, Africa, Germany, Hawaii, the South Pacific, and even California.

Some poor folks who'd never had two dimes to rub together were advised that before too long they'd be coming into some money. About the same time as the ones who got to travel were leaving town, these people began collecting fat paychecks from the Aero Supply, Raymond Manufacturing, The Corry-Jamestown and Rogers Steel, all located in Corry, all making things to fight the war with.

One other important fact about Mrs. McGee; she was the only person in Spring Creek Township who was a member of the WCDPC (Warren County Democratic Party Committee)! Because she was an important Democrat, Mrs. McGee thought very highly of President Roosevelt. LR, as you may recall, did not. Many times when she was at the store to buy groceries they'd discuss the matter quite loudly. Once I heard her tell LR she found it hard to believe a boy as smart as he had been in grade school could have grown up to be so ignorant about certain things.

I guess the only other thing to say about Mrs. McGee is that she was the only grown-up lady I ever knew who rode down the Blue Eye Hill road on a bobsled and knew the right thing to do when the driver hollered, "Roll off!"

# Eight
## "Roll Off!"

From mid-December until late February the steep, winding, mile-long, one-lane, and little-traveled Blue Eye Hill road was just about the best bobsledding place in all of Western Pennsylvania. It might well have been the best except that it intersected with Corry-Garland road and then crossed the Pennsylvania Railroad tracks before bottoming out on the Brokenstraw Creek Bridge. It's true not many cars or trains passed through Spring Creek during the 1930's; however there was always that chance, and not many bobsledders wanted to end up under the wheels of one or the other. Because there's no way to quickly stop a speeding bobsled other than tipping it over, that's what was required just after coming around the curve in front of the church.

Incidentally, the bobsled we're talking about here wasn't much like the fancy ones with steering wheels and brakes used in the Winter Olympics. The Blue Eye bobsled was a ten- or twelve-foot wooden plank about a foot and a half wide with wooden runners attached underneath. The front runners were on a swivel and were steered with a piece of rope.

A Blue Eye bobsled with four or five riders on board rounding that curve by the church would be traveling at least twenty-five, thirty or even more miles an hour. (When sitting a few inches above the ground it seemed more like a hundred.) Crashing a loaded bobsled traveling at that speed without badly injuring or permanently disfiguring the riders required a brave and experienced bobsled driver and riders who responded immediately when the driver shouted, "Roll off!" Hearing that, the riders had to instantly let go of the plank and lean so far over they'd fall onto the road. By doubling up their legs and sliding

down the road on their backs they avoided serious damage to themselves or what they were wearing. Inexperienced riders sometimes ended up on their stomachs, not a good thing because the road's rough and icy surface removed buttons, hats, gloves, and/or small patches of skin from faces and hands.

Seconds after telling the riders to "roll off," the driver pulled the front runners sharply to the right causing the bobsled to skid off the road, traverse a shallow ditch and climb a steep snow covered bank. About half way to the top, the driver jumped off just before the bobsled tipped over and slid back down the bank. After that came the hard job of pulling the heavy bobs back to the top of the hill, and volunteering to help was one sure way to get a Blue Eye bobsled ride.

One Saturday morning in January the Blue Eye road was completely iced over because the traditional January thaw had been followed by an abrupt and steep drop in temperature. The word about this ideal surface quickly spread and by 10:00 A.M. most of the Spring Creek area's bobsledders were hard at it. This happened to be the day the new city boy, Zeke, whose family had just moved from Corry to a nearby farm, showed up at the Blue Eye for the first time. Coming from the city, he was much taken by the speed and noise of the bobsleds, so he quickly volunteered to help pull Bobby Crane's bobs up the hill.

The Blue Eye Hill was also great for sledding. A lightweight sled with one person on it was much slower and far less frightening than a bobsled. Plus you didn't have to roll off onto the hard, icy road at the end of the ride. That's why I was on the hill that day with my good old Western Flier, and I happened to be pulling it up past the church just as Bobby and his four riders came thundering around the curve. The new boy, eyes squeezed shut, was at the very back since that was supposedly the safest place for first-time riders. When Bobby shouted, "Roll off!" the three experienced riders in front of Zeke quickly ended up on their backs sliding down the icy road. The trouble was nobody had thought to tell Zeke about the business of rolling off so he maintained his tight hold on the plank. Bobby, believing everybody had gone overboard, aimed for the ditch and the bobsled headed up the steep bank. What happened when Bobby himself jumped off surprised everybody except Zeke, inasmuch as his eyes were squeezed tightly shut and he didn't know the bobsled was supposed to tip over.

It was no doubt Zeke's weight at the very back of the bobsled which caused it to spin around and head straight back down the bank. It promptly picked up speed gaining more than enough momentum to re-cross the ditch and pop back up onto the icy road. There, the front runners took the course of least resistance and turned the bobsled back down the Blue Eye Hill road towards the intersection and the railroad crossing. However, the warning lights were now flashing, meaning a train was coming.

A few seconds later the bobsled and Zeke zipped through the Corry-Garland intersection and the railroad crossing was just a couple of hundred feet further down the hill. From where he stood in front of the church it seemed to Bobby that he was seeing the last of his toboggan, while the rest of us thought we were seeing the last of Zeke. At that moment the nose of the engine appeared from behind the embankment at the left; however it was moving slowly. Then, just before it reached the crossing, the train jolted to a complete stop. A split second later Zeke and the bobsled flashed a few feet in front of the engine's cowcatcher.

The train was the "local," used for short freight hauls between Corry and Warren. Every week or so it stopped in Spring Creek to drop or pick up a tank car at the milk plant, or a box car at the feedmill. Some days, and fortunately for Bobby and Zeke, this happened to be one of them, the local stopped even when it didn't need to. This was so the engineer could send the brakeman, Mr. Theobold, up to the store for a pound of the extra sharp New York State cheese which the engineer favored. In a manner of speaking Zeke's life was saved by a piece of cheese.

After the near miss the bobsled gradually slowed, stopping just past the Brokenstraw bridge. Zeke got off, picked up the rope and began dragging it back up the hill. By the time Bobby and the rest of us met up with Zeke he'd gotten as far as the railroad crossing where the engineer was standing waiting for him. The engineer, who thought Zeke had done what he did on purpose, was pretty mad at him for almost having run into his train. He made Zeke swear right then and there he'd never do it again, and you can say this about Zeke if nothing else: he kept his word. In fact he wanted to keep his word so bad he never again caught a ride on a bobsled down the Blue Eye.

# Nine
## The Talent Show

Every June the Ladies Aid Society put on the Spring Creek Township Annual Talent Show at the Community Building. You can laugh when I say this, but there were a lot of talented people living in or near Spring Creek, and each year the show was at least as good as it had been the year before. Mostly because about the same people were in it. Nevertheless, it was well worth the price of admission which was free unless you counted putting something in the Ladies Aid Society's Poor Box.

When the last act was over, the contestants lined up on the platform and the people in the audience voted for their favorite by raising their hands when he, she, or it was asked to step forward by the MC. I've already said Mrs. McGee usually won first prize because she was a good whistler and bird imitator, but that's not saying the other contestants didn't give her a good run for the money. Mr. Johnson was usually a close second since he was the best singer in the church choir and a lot of folks thought he sounded pretty much like Nelson Eddy when he sang "Stout Hearted Men," and "Indian Love Call." Mary Jane Cole drew quite a few votes wearing and singing about her "Sweet Little Alice Blue Gown." Uncle Lon was also a favorite, being as he was a one man band playing a clarinet, a piano, and a violin. (Not at the same time, of course.) Mr. Mead and the three-man West Spring Creek Square Dance Band got most of the farmers' votes doing hillbilly songs. Good looking Mervy Shacks, who could play the mouth organ and guitar at the same time, always got quite a few votes from the ladies.

The other regular contestants, the old man from Piccadilly Hill who played music blowing on empty jugs while he strummed a washboard; the Kowowski sisters who folk-danced; and little

Dickie Carr who played the accordion, were all pretty good but most years only their close relatives voted for them. (Dickie would probably have done better if he could have played more songs than "Lady of Spain," and "The Pennsylvania Polka.")

One year the Society put Ma in charge of lining up the talent for the show which usually wasn't much of a job as long as you had the list of who'd been in it last time. However, that was the year Uncle Lon had hurt his hand at the feed mill; the Kowowski sisters' family had moved to Ohio; and the jug-and-washboard man had died. Ma was having a tough time filling all those empty slots and was getting desperate. So much so she thought maybe I could play my sweet potato (ocarina) and Grampa Charley a mouth organ. After a couple practice sessions she decided against that.

One of LR's favorite radio programs was Edgar Bergen and Charlie McCarthy, which is how Ma got the idea about me being a dummy that would sit on Grampa Charley's knee and say things while Grampa Charley made his lips move. M. and H. (older sisters) agreed I would be a very good dummy since I already had lots of practice. Ma and Aunt Martha wrote what we were supposed to say, and Grampa Charley and I practiced every evening for a week. My older sisters complained about it and called us "Chubby and Morty" (Mortimer Snerd was the hayseed dummy on Edgar Bergen's show). Which was why Grampa Charley named our act "Chubby and Morty."

The night of the show Ma dressed me in a sort of clown suit (made out of old long johns) and put white powder and rouge on my face. When it was our turn, the preacher's wife, who was the master of ceremonies, said she was very excited about this new ventriloquist act, Mr. Chubby and dummy, Morty. She said we'd most likely end up in Hollywood.

I was too big for Grampa Charley to carry so from our front row seats he dragged me by the arms up the two steps onto the temporary stage. Then he sat down in a chair, lifted me onto his lap and said, "Well, Morty, here we are in beautiful downtown Spring Creek at the Ladies Aid Talent Show. Is there anything you want to say to the audience?"

In the squeaky voice Ma told me I should use I said, with Grampa Charley moving his lips at the same time, "Is there a carpenter in the house?"

Chubby: "Why in the world do you care if there's a carpenter in the house?"

Morty: "Because I think you broke my legs dragging me onto the stage." (Laughter)

Then Grampa Charley (Chubby) said, "Morty, your legs are just fine and we've got an act to put on here. Don't you know how hurt all these people would feel if I had to tell them our act was canceled because your legs were broken?"

Morty: "Only their hands would hurt because they'd clap them so hard!" (Laughter)

Chubby: "Say, Morty; what about that lady announcing we might go to Hollywood?"

Morty: "That was no lady; that was the preacher's wife! (Laughter) And I didn't like it because she called me a dummy."

Chubby: "But you are a dummy! Why don't you want to be called a dummy?"

Morty: "Because everybody will think I'm a Republican!" (Laughter and applause) (Mrs. McGee clapped the hardest.)

From there the jokes got even worse. On the other hand, I was good at swiveling my head around and rolling my eyes and Grampa Charley made his lips move just right. That's probably why we won first prize. Or maybe it was what we did last. Grampa Charley, to prove what a good ventriloquist he was, drank a glass of water while I sang "Good Night Ladies."

Mrs. McGee only got second prize that night but didn't mind it one bit. She said it was worth losing just to hear the Republican joke. Ma thought we'd been just wonderful. LR said the reason we'd won first prize was because the audience must have thought we were really good actors to put on such a really bad act.

# Ten

# Muley Richards Upstages Santa

Don't think for a minute there weren't some pretty big events in Spring Creek even if it was a small town. For example, there was the Annual Memorial Day parade when LR and the other World War One veterans squeezed into their old uniforms and, along with Boy Scout Troop 92, a drum and bugle band from the Corry Veterans' Club, and a bunch of kids with American flags riding on a horse-drawn wagon, marched out to the cemetery to put flags on dead soldiers' graves. Another big event was the last-day-of-school picnic at the end of April when moms brought bowls of stuff to eat, the store donated Kool-Aid and rainbow ice cream packets, and there was a softball game against the West Spring Creek Grade School.

The biggest happening of the year, however, was the annual Christmas play in which every one of the fifty or so kids in the school's eight grades had a part. The three teachers made this happen by rewriting the script to include actors, songs, dances and other things the author hadn't thought about. On the Friday night the play was shown at the Congregational Church, every pew was filled to overflowing with parents, grandparents, aunts, uncles, and other relatives of the cast members.

A day or two after the Thanksgiving vacation all the kids were jammed into the Middle room where Miss Allen taught the fourth, fifth, and sixth grades. There we'd be told what the Christmas play was about that year, and each of us received a piece of paper saying who or what we were going to be. Who or what depended on how old or how big you were and if you were smart or not smart. Also, the teachers knew pretty well which kids could carry a tune, and who could walk three steps without tripping over their own feet. These were the ones picked to be the singers and dancers. The teachers also gave everyone a note to take home to their Ma's because everybody had to have a costume and somebody had to make them.

It might seem that making a costume in time for the dress rehearsal would have been a difficult job, but back then and back there, it wasn't. In those years, particularly in that corner of northwest Pennsylvania, the answer to the long, cold winters, partially heated houses, and drafty schoolrooms, was woolen long winter underwear (long johns) and long cotton or wool stockings. Nearly every man, woman and child, from the youngest to the oldest, townfolks as well as farmfolks, was outfitted with at least one pair of each which, after several winters, would be worn out or outgrown by the last growing member of the family. When the raggedy and outgrown long johns were patched up, dyed the right color, and fitted out with painted cardboard buttons and such, they became very believable attire for elves, brownies, toy soldiers, Raggedy Ann dolls, reindeer and most of the other characters in the play. The only exceptions were the singers in the Snow Flake Choir who in their long john costumes looked more like lumpy, gray snowballs than snowflakes.

Of course not everybody in the cast got to wear dyed woolen underwear. Angels, when they were in the cast, wore white sparkly robes so their costumes were made from bed sheets with little silver colored stars glued on them. The kids who were Christmas toys, blocks, jack-in-the-boxes, and such, were put in painted cardboard boxes with their arms and legs sticking out. Angels' wings, the toy soldiers' guns, reindeer antlers and such as that were also made from the cardboard boxes provided free of charge by LR's store.

For the first two weeks after Thanksgiving each group rehearsed an hour a day, the singers and dancers in the Middle Room where Miss Allen's piano was; the actors upstairs in the Big Room; and the toy soldiers, brownies, elves and so forth in the Little Room. During the second two weeks, school was closed an hour early each day and we'd be marched down the schoolhouse road to practice at the church. The play was performed there inasmuch as it was the only building in town with a stage and which was large enough to hold all the kids' relatives. At the church, where it was always very cold, we'd be made to sit quietly on the hard pews when we weren't part of the group practicing on the stage. Practicing at the church wasn't something you looked forward to.

On the Tuesday of the last week of play practice, everyone had to bring in their costumes and cardboard accessories. Some of the ladies from the PTA (Parent-Teachers Association), and the Spring Creek Ladies Aid Society would be at the church with their scissors, and pins and needles to take care of whatever needed fixing, and by Wednesday costuming would have been pretty well completed. This was a good thing because dress rehearsal was the next day, the Thursday before the Friday performance.

The dress rehearsal was exciting. Everybody got to dress up, and the full orchestra was there to practice along with the dancers and singers. Until then the music at the church had been just Miss Allen on the church's old upright piano, but now she was accompanied by Uncle Lon, who played both the violin and the clarinet (not at the same time), Miss Jackson on the church's pump organ, and Mrs. McGee with her tambourine and castanets. Another reason dress rehearsal was exciting was because, for the benefit of the orchestra, there'd be a fire going in the wood-burning stove.

For dress rehearsal all the necessary furniture would be on the stage, most of it loaned by the Eddys and the Maxwells who lived near church. The handmade props, maybe a fireplace, a grandfather's clock, a front door, or a sleigh, were also in place. The props were made from cardboard or plywood or both, by some of the kids' dads. They could make anything that was needed, even the smoking volcano used one year.

The volcano was required so that in addition to bringing toys for the kids on a tropical island, Santa could give the grownup natives the thing they wanted most for Christmas, a volcano that wouldn't someday blow up. To make the volcano seem more ominous, one of the kids' dads who worked at the milk plant volunteered to make it smoke. To do this he sat inside the volcano and mixed some special chemicals borrowed from the milk plant, namely hydrochloric acid and ammonia, which produce a dense white smoke-like cloud when they get near each other.

At the dress rehearsal the volcano, with the smoke-making dad inside, performed very well for the short time it was tested. However during the play when he had to remain hidden in the volcano for all of act two, the acid and ammonia fumes got so bad inside that the dad had to frequently stick his head out of the top to breathe. It was peculiar to see a head pop out of the smoking volcano, however most of the audience thought it was the evil volcano god the tribal chief had previously told Santa about.

Considering the large number of children in the play, and the very broad range of their singing, dancing, acting and thinking capabilities, it would seem such unscheduled events as the head in the volcano would be the rule rather than the exception. The reason they were not was that the teachers excelled at organizing, directing and producing the plays. None the less, they couldn't control every little thing, which is why Muley, the elf, managed to so badly upstage Santa one year. As well as everybody else on the stage.

The basic theme of that year's play was Santa Claus ate too much while making his rounds, got sick and collapsed to the floor while delivering toys to the Smith children. He'd been forewarned by Mrs. Claus this could happen, but Santa laughed, "Ho, ho, ho," and said he couldn't disappoint children by not eating what they'd put out for him.

The Snowflake Singers made it clear to the audience that by the time he arrived at the Smiths' house, Santa had visited a number of countries around the world and had eaten lots of different stuff. While putting the Smith children's toys under their tree and eating Mrs. Smith's nut fudge brownies, he suddenly fell to the floor with a loud thump. Hearing the noise, the three Smith children woke up, rushed onto the stage to find Santa lying there, and called for their parents. When Mr. Smith saw Santa Claus he began running in circles saying how terrible it all was. Mrs. Smith, who was better at dealing with things like this, told one of the children to run next door and fetch good Dr. Goode; he'd know what to do.

Dr. Goode hurried on-stage wearing a white smock and carrying a large doctor's bag, which was really one of his Ma's old purses painted white with a red cross taped on it. He was followed by several neighborhood children who'd heard the commotion, plus a couple reindeer and three elves. A doll and a toy soldier from beneath the tree magically came to life and joined the crowd around Santa because they were also very worried about him. All together there was a large group of cast members on the stage when what happened did.

After examining Santa with his stethoscope, Good Doctor Goode announced to everybody that Santa was alive but needed an operation, otherwise he might burst. Then the three elves, the toy soldier, and Mr. Smith, who had stopped running in circles, were supposed to lift Fat Walter—that is to say, Santa Claus—onto a table. From behind a back-lighted sheet held up between the table and the audience by the two reindeer, Dr. Goode was then to pretend, using a wood saw, hedge clippers and large tongs, to perform the operation. The audience would see shadows of things being removed inside Santa, including cheese from Sweden, fish from Norway; oranges from California, sausages from Germany, and apples from New Zealand.

Because of the momentous seriousness of the situation, the actors and audience were all very quiet as the three elves, the tall but skinny toy soldier, and the eleven-year-old Mr. Smith began to lift Santa from the floor. Dr. Goode whispered loudly they must "be very careful so he doesn't burst!" Fat Walter (Santa) was no lightweight, and picking him up was no easy chore. In fact, it was too much for Muley Richards, and it was he who burst, not Santa Claus.

Muley came from an especially poor farm family that ate lots of baked beans and wild leeks. A wild leek, in case you don't know, is a big, very strong onion. Undoubtedly that had been Muley's supper a couple hours before the play, and such foods, in case you don't know, produce lots of gas when being digested. In that quiet and solemn moment as they struggled to lift Fat Walter, the gas escaped loudly from Muley's raised posterior. The actors were quickly enveloped in an invisible but extremely bad-smelling and eye-watering cloud of digested leek and bean fumes.

Except for Muley, the Santa lifters all released their hold on him and beat a fast retreat to the far side of the stage where they were quickly joined by the other actors. Muley retained his hold on Santa, but only until Santa speedily recovered, wrenched free from his grip and joined the others across the stage, wiping his eyes with his white beard.

Miss Henry, in the curtained-off area back stage, immediately got a whiff of the problem and frantically motioned the curtain pullers to draw them shut. As soon as they were closed she marched on stage and whispered loudly for everybody to return immediately to the positions they'd held before Muley's "indiscretion." (Her words.) By then the air had cleared only just enough that this was possible. The curtains parted, and this time Santa made it onto the operating table. The operation was successful, a feat which the children, toys, reindeer, elves and the rest of the cast celebrated in the concluding song, "Good Doctor Goode Saves Santa." Which I think was the name of the play.

There were four curtain calls that night, and each time it was when Muley and the other elves stepped forward that the audience clapped the loudest.

# Eleven
## The Brokenstraw

Before they could cool their milk with electricity, farmers had to have some way to keep the milk from going sour before they took it to the milk plant. Most of them kept their milk cans in cement tubs filled with cold running spring water inside a small building called a milk-house. You need to know this if you want to learn anything about the Brokenstraw Creek. It starts in a milk-house on a farm up near Clymer, New York. (At least it did sixty years ago.)

Water overflows from the cement tubs, seeps through the boards in the floor and trickles from underneath to form a small stream which heads south toward Pennsylvania. By the time it's meandered the twelve miles to the state line it's gathered enough water from other streams and brooks to become the Brokenstraw Creek.

A few miles into Pennsylvania the Brokenstraw flows through the town of Columbus and a bit further on it's joined by Hare Creek which comes from near the city of Corry. This wasn't such a good thing before Corry got a sewage treatment plant because Hare Creek was where the flushes from all of the city of Corry's bathrooms went. A mile past where it meets with Hare Creek the Brokenstraw makes a sharp left turn and heads east by southeast.

Five miles later the waters of the Brokenstraw and Hare Creek, plus, back then, whatever else Hare Creek had to offer, run through the middle of the town of Spring Creek. After veering behind where the blacksmith shop was located and passing beneath the bridge to West Spring Creek, the Brokenstraw flows near where the tannery used to be. Just before it leaves town, it flows past where there was once an old wooden dam and mill

53

pond, and after that it's on its way to Garland, Pittsfield, Youngsville and Irvine. Near Irvine it joins the mighty Allegheny River and heads for Pittsburgh.

Some people not raised in the Brokenstraw valley think Brokenstraw is a peculiar name for a creek. So do a lot of people who were raised there. Something you may not know is that when democrat, Franklin D. Roosevelt, was president, LR and the other township supervisors, all Republicans, wanted to change the name of the Brokenstraw to Roosevelt Creek. They wanted to do this because in their opinion, President Roosevelt was as full of it as was the Brokenstraw. (Because of Hare Creek.)

Nobody's really sure about where the name did come from, but some old-timer Spring Creekers claimed it was because from on top of a hill the sharp left turn it makes between Corry and Spring Creek looks like a broken straw. That doesn't make a lot of sense because there is no hill where you can see that bend from. Other old-timers said that Brokenstraw came from the Indian word "awbrowkhensraw" which Indians had used to describe the creek. "Awbrowkhensraw," loosely translated, meant "don't drink the water." This probably isn't true either. In order for Indians to have known not to drink the water they would had to have lived along the creek after Corry became a city and before the city did anything about all their toilets dumping into Hare Creek. As far as anybody knows, by that time the Indians had all moved to Erie or someplace.

Most of the year the Brokenstraw was a great place to catch fish; bullheads, trout, and bass, which were good to eat, and shiners, sheepheads, suckers, and carp which were not. You could also occasionally hook onto a mud puppy, big nasty looking lizards with teeth. When a mud puppy took your bait, you usually could count on it taking your hook, line, bobber and sinker as well.

The first day of trout season was always April 15th. After that about every night after school and on most Sundays, most of us little guys would head for the Brokenstraw with our bamboo poles and coffee cans of nightcrawlers. By the way, nightcrawler hunting is a sport just like fishing and about as much fun. If you've never done it, give it a try. Get a flashlight and an empty coffee can (coffee cans are taller so nightcrawlers have a harder time crawling out) and go out after dark in people's yards, especially if the grass is wet. (Do not try this in yards where the people in the house have guns and might think you're a burglar.) Shine your light around and you're bound to spot a lot of fat worms, about three to five inches long. These are nightcrawlers which come out after dark to lie around on the grass, and, when they're in the mood, make love to another nightcrawler.

It's what a nightcrawler does when you try to pick it up that makes a nightcrawler hunt an exciting sport. When it crawls from the ground at night it stretches itself out but always keeps one of its two ends, believed to be the back end, tucked inside the hole it came from. (Except for the ones making love; they usually forget about doing this.) When a nightcrawler gets even the slightest suspicion that anything or anybody is planning to grab it, it instantly shrinks itself way down and in a split second disappears back into the hole. The trick to catching one is to slowly place your thumb and forefinger on either side of it just above the hole it's got its behind in. Very quickly pinch them together, and, if you're fast enough, you may have caught yourself a nightcrawler! Nightcrawlers are slimy and slippery as well as being quick; therefore, just like trout, they often get away.

Something important to remember is when you've got a good hold on one, you must slowly and carefully drag it from the hole since he or she will be hanging on for dear life and you don't want to pull it in two. That is, if you're planning to go trout fishing. Bass and bullheads don't mind your using half a nightcrawler, but if you want to catch a trout you'll need a nightcrawler which is whole and in good health. It takes quite awhile to become good at nightcrawling, so at first keep your eyes open for the ones making love; it's not really fair, but they're easy to catch and you can sometimes catch two at a time. You won't collect enough of these lover types to fill a coffee can but you will get enough to go fishing for awhile.

Everybody had their favorite fishing places on the Brokenstraw. Mine were along the bank beside the road out to Tuffy's farm; by the outlet from the milk plant; and near the remains of the wooden damn down past the old tannery. The bank by the road to Tuffy's was good because most evenings after supper, older boys and men would fish there, and listening to them talk and carry on, us younger fellows could learn swear words and dirty stories. Also, there weren't many trees or bushes so it was a place where you could throw out your hook and line and not have it end up in a tree. Same thing if you caught anything; when you jerked a fish out of the water, it wouldn't get hung up on a branch.

The place where the pipe from the milk plant poured out left-over powdered milk and other stuff into the creek was the place to fish if you wanted to be sure to catch something. The trouble was mostly what you caught were suckers, carp and shiners, fish not many folks wanted to eat because they were too bony and hard to clean. About the only way to eat a carp was to nail it to a pine board, boil it for an hour, then throw the carp away and eat the board. That's an old Spring Creek joke.

The best place to catch a trout was in the deep hole, the old mill pond, just below the old dam. Here's where you had to know what you were doing because trout are particular about what they want to eat and when they want to eat it. You also had to be careful because trees were all around waiting to capture your hook and line, or a flying fish when you jerked it too hard from the water. It seemed like every time this happened to me, a fisherman would walk by and ask, "How's the fishin' up thar?"

When I was seven it was by the dam where I caught my first major-sized trout, an eighteen-inch rainbow. After untangling it from the tree, I didn't even take it off the hook but ran the half-mile back to our house with the fish dangling from the end of the pole so I could show Ma. Of course Ma was very excited about it, saying she couldn't remember seeing a bigger one, and at supper time she cooked it for LR and me. LR said it was about time somebody else in the family helped bring home the bacon!

Fishing wasn't the only thing the Brokenstraw was good for. Many winters the creek would freeze all the way across, except where there were riffles and rapids, which made it good for ice skating and ice fishing. When the winter was especially cold the ice would be as much as five or six inches thick in some places, and then, in early spring when it broke up, there was "chunk riding." What you did was find a long stick and a good sized cake (a chunk) of ice floating in a back water or stuck on low hanging bushes. You'd jump on the chunk, use the stick to push it out to where the water was flowing faster, then ride down as far as the old dam. Here, where the creek had to squeeze between the old wooden pilings, you jumped off, which you had to do if you didn't want to end up in Garland or Pittsburgh or someplace. The ice chunk would float over the dam and you hiked back upstream to find another one to ride back down.

Except during the spring floods, the Brokenstraw wasn't deep enough even for rowboats since in most places the oars would scrape the bottom and bang into rocks. As for rafting, that could also be done in times of high water, but it's certainly something I wouldn't recommend. (See next chapter.)

# Twelve

## Rafting on the Brokenstraw (Not Recommended)

April was usually a soggy month in Spring Creek, but in 1938 the rain outdid itself. From the first day of the month through the fifteenth when trout season opened it rained hard and long every single day, and, just as Aunt Hat said, the raindrops were "big as horse turds." The Brokenstraw Creek that year rose higher than anybody could remember and it was more than three weeks after trout season opened before you could get close enough to fish in it. There wasn't much to do around Spring Creek in April if you couldn't go fishing, which is why I volunteered to peck potatoes at the store for two cents a bag. That's how I learned about rafting on the Brokenstraw.

At the far end of the store's cold, dank and dim cellar was a large wooden bin where potatoes bought from farmers were stored. Next to the bin was a platform scale and to peck potatoes you put a brown paper bag on the scale and filled it with fifteen pounds of potatoes. People bought potatoes by the peck in those days, and if you don't think pecking a bag of potatoes was worth two cents and more, you never did it.

First of all, when potatoes have been stored for awhile some get rotten, and nothing smells worse than rotten potatoes except rotten cabbage. All the rotten ones had to be sorted out, put in a barrow and wheeled to the burn pile behind the store. Secondly, the potatoes were delivered to the store just as they came from the ground, dirty, and before you could bag it each and every potato had to be wiped off with a stiff brush. Third, the fifteen-pound peck bags of potatoes had to be carried back through the cellar, up the long wooden steps, and stacked neatly in front of the hardware counter. If all that didn't make it worth two cents, I don't know what would.

Near the potato bin, where it was out of the sight of most people, LR kept a barrel of hard cider, reserved for certain customers like Mr. Bates, Mr. Potemski and old Mr. Wagner. One afternoon while I was pecking, those three were over by the barrel drinking cider out of tin cups. They were talking about the days when they'd ridden log rafts on the Brokenstraw.

That was back when trees in the hills around Spring Creek were big enough to make into boards. During the winter, maples, oaks, and hickories were chopped down and dragged to the edge of the Brokenstraw by teams of horses. In early spring when the Brokenstraw was running full, the logs were rolled into the creek, floated down to the mill pond below the dam and tied together to make rafts. Old Mr. Wagner, Mr. Bates and Mr. Potemski were a lot younger back then, and they got paid to ride the rafts all the way down to where the Brokenstraw meets the Allegheny River, about six miles west of Warren. There they'd sell the log rafts to men who made them into bigger log rafts and floated them down the Allegheny to Pittsburgh. After that the three of them hiked on to Warren to see the bright lights, visit saloons and attend to ladies of the night. They sometimes stayed overnight at the Allegheny Hotel if they hadn't got put in jail for being in a fight, and the next day or so, hopped a freight train for the ride back to Spring Creek.

Being only eleven years old with a Ma who was a church deacon, I, of course, wasn't much interested in what the three men had to say about bright lights, saloons or night ladies. (I didn't even know what a night lady was.) On the other hand, I was very interested in what they said about riding a raft down the Brokenstraw, inasmuch as it certainly sounded very much like something that should be done one day. By chance, that one day happened only one week later.

By the end of the next week the Brokenstraw was still high and running swift, however was back within its banks. Saturday morning, pole and nightcrawler can in hand, I set off for the place by the dam where the year before I'd caught that monster trout. Before I left, Ma made me promise not to get close to the water because I would no doubt fall in and get washed away. I crossed my heart and hoped to die I wouldn't, even though I knew you couldn't fish unless you were standing next to the creek.

The ground around the old mill pond below the dam was wet and mushy; not a good place to stand while you were fishing. However, near there floating next to the bank held by some partly immersed willow bushes, I discovered an eight- or ten-foot square section of what had been a wooden bridge. It must have washed away during the flood and now it looked like an ideal platform from which to fish. Clutching my pole and can of nightcrawlers, I jumped from the bank, landing on the rear of the platform which caused the platform to break free from the bushes and I was accidentally rafting on the Brokenstraw.

At first my raft and I drifted slowly and smoothly across the old millpond toward the opposite bank where I planned to de-bark as soon as we were close enough. Unfortunately, about halfway across the current began to push the raft downstream toward the pond's outlet, a narrow channel between two high banks. The raft began moving faster; then, after entering the channel, began to pitch and roll and bump into rocks. By sitting in the center of the raft and wedging my fingers through cracks between the boards I was able to stay aboard. Twice the raft brushed against one of the creek's rocky banks, but jumping off was out of the question since I wasn't about to let go of those boards.

After a couple of minutes the creek began to widen again and the raft gradually slowed to a reasonable speed. Now it was only my stomach that was pitching and rolling. Then I felt the raft begin to surge forward again as it approached another chan-nel of boiling water. This time the rapids were worse and to keep from being tossed into the creek I had to lie face down and hold tightly onto the planks. Which isn't easy to do with very wet, cold fingers. Waves washed over the raft soaking me from top to bottom, and I was closer to the water than Ma could have imagined.

Again the steep banks on either side of the narrow channel backed away and for the second time the raft floating onto a fairly long and straight stretch of smooth water. Ahead I could see the Cemetery Road bridge and immediately hoped somebody had died so there'd be a funeral procession at whose members I could yell for help. A few minutes later the unoccupied bridge was passed overhead and just beyond that is where the Brokenstraw is joined by the Spring Creek creek. It was also brimful of water so now the Brokenstraw became wider and deeper, and the next rapids we hit were longer, rougher, and rockier than ever. Hanging on not only became more difficult, it also became more important. I didn't recall old Mr. Wagner, Mr. Bates and Mr. Potemski saying one thing about having to hang on for dear life even though you were wet, cold, and sick at your stomach; and afraid.

As we went beneath the second bridge, the one the politicians used to get to the Henry farm, I mentally counted the bridges we'd be passing under before the raft reached the Allegheny River. Bridges where maybe I might be able to attract somebody's attention to my predicament. There were only five before the Brokenstraw flowed into the Allegheny River beyond Irvine; one in Garland, one in Pittsfield, two in Youngsville, and one in Irvine.

While fretting about this, I heard a low rumble which at first I thought might be a train since the Brokenstraw ran not far from and parallel to the railroad tracks. However, the rumble soon developed into a fairly loud roar which was apparently coming from further ahead on the Brokenstraw. The raft surged eagerly forward as it rounded the next curve, and there was a narrow gorge filled with the swiftest, steepest and roughest rapids I'd ever seen, except at Niagara Falls. This time the raft didn't just rock and roll, it bucked and lunged. Instead of just bumping into rocks, it crashed against them, each crash spinning the raft in circles. I lost my grip on the boards several times but fortunately was able to get another hold before sliding overboard. That definitely would not have been a good thing to do. The can of nightcrawlers had disappeared during the first set of rapids; the fishing pole during the second, and I seriously believed I'd be next.

The raft was moving very fast when suddenly the narrow gorge veered sharply to the right. However, due to its speed and weight, the raft missed the turn and plunged straight ahead. A moment later it ground to a complete stop on a narrow ledge of rock and gravel jutting from the bank into the creek. It took a second for me to realize what had happened and another second to take advantage of it. I leaped onto the ledge, falling face first into a shallow pool of cold, gray muck. Don't think for a moment I cared.

At the top of the bank was a barbed wire fence over which a cow was peering down at me with seeming interest. While it's true what they say about most cows—they look pretty much alike—this one had four big protruding front teeth. That's why Fat Walter had named her, his 4H project cow, "Bucky." I had washed up near Fat Walter's dad's farm, two miles from Spring Creek.

With Bucky tagging along, I set out for Fat Walter's house, getting there just in time to catch Fat Walter and his pa getting into their truck to pick up grain at the feedmill. His pa said he'd mistook me for a beaver, being as wet and muddy as I was, and asked where the Hell had I come from. I told him about the raft ride, and told Fat Walter he could have the raft if he wanted it. His pa said no, he couldn't.

I was such a mess Fat Walter's pa made me ride in the back of the truck to Spring Creek. He pulled up by the store to drop me off, and who should be coming out the front door but Ma. She immediately hit me with a barrage of questions, so many I could hardly make up answers fast enough. Why hadn't I come home for lunch? Why was I so wet and muddy? Where was my fishing pole? And, why had she seen me get out of Fat Walter's pa's truck?

I answered every single question honestly. After I got down to the dam to fish I just kept moving down the creek until I suddenly realized I'd gone as far as Fat Walter's pa's farm. I was all wet by getting splashed because the creek was running fast and high. I'd gotten muddy climbing up the bank and crawling under the barbed-wire fence. As for the missing pole, it fell in the creek, and since she said I shouldn't get too close to the water I couldn't get it back.

As you know, honesty is the best policy. She soon got over being upset because I had missed lunch and come home looking such a mess. I, on the other hand never got over the raft ride on the Brokenstraw. Which is why I never went on another one, and why I don't recommend it as something to do on the Brokenstraw.

# Thirteen
# Lefty and Adolph

Just across the Brokenstraw Creek bridge a dirt road to the left went out to the Morton farm and not far beyond it, the dilapidated brick house where Old Mrs. Davidson lived. Old Mr. Davidson didn't live there, being as he'd up and walked out on old Mrs. Davidson the day she gave away his hunting dog, Sarge. Only because Sarge had eaten a rooster and five of her settin' hens.

Half way to the Morton farm, near where the road went over the spillway from Morton's Pond to the Brokenstraw, a short path led up a slight rise to the door of a small tarpaper-covered shack. On one side of the path was a long handled water pump; on the other a black iron kettle hung over a stone-lined fire pit. Off to the right firewood was stacked near the edge of the bank above the pond, and behind the shack near the edge of the woods was a narrow hut with FRONT OFFICE painted on the door. It was a backhouse.

Inside the shack a small potbellied wood stove stood near the wall on the right, and beyond it, a narrow wooden table and stool. Along the left wall was a short plywood counter and wooden sink which drained to the outside through a piece of gutter pipe. Past the sink sat a frayed wicker rocking chair, and across the rear of the shack, beneath a wide plywood shelf was a narrow cot. Like the plank floor, the cot was covered with deer hides. Piled on the shelf above the cot were jackets, boots, caps, a couple rifles, three holstered pistols of various calibers, several fishing poles, animal traps, frog-spearing forks and other items too numerous to mention. A kerosene lantern swung over the table, an old Motorola table radio sat on the counter, and a few pans and cups hung from hooks on the wall above the sink.

There was no icebox; whatever had to be kept cool was down in the pond in wire baskets.

The tarpaper shack was where Lefty and Adolph lived, Lefty being one of Spring Creek's best known citizens, and Adolph the hunting dog old Mrs. Davidson had given to Lefty the day Sarge had consumed her chickens. The dog had a thatch of brown hair falling over one eye and a small strip of black underneath his big nose. Lefty thought it made him look like the dictator over in Germany so he changed Sarge's name to Adolph.

It may not seem that Lefty and Adolph's shack would have been such a great place to live, but nearly every Spring Creek boy looked forward to the day when he could move into one just like it. While waiting for that day to arrive, we were regular visitors at Lefty's because where else could you learn more about hunting, trapping, fishing, spearing frogs, and girls? Or see the pictures of pretty much undressed girls from *Esquire Magazine* pinned up on the wall behind the stove? When the weather was good, we'd loaf outside, sitting around the fire pit where Lefty was usually cooking something or boiling his dirty clothes in the black iron pot. On rainy and wintry days we crowded inside, soaking up the heat from the wood-stove and inhaling the very agreeable aroma of wood smoke, kerosene, wet dog, deer skins, fried leeks and Lefty's pipe.

Lefty was probably the best hunter in Warren County, and chunks of venison, rabbit, coon, possum, squirrel, duck, or pheasant were usually bubbling in the kettle. Oh, yes; also rattlesnake, one of Lefty's favorite suppers. He was also an expert fisherman, knowing just where and when to bait up with slugs, nightcrawlers, cheese balls or flies to catch brown trout, rainbow trout, bass or bullheads. Lefty was also a good trapper, so each winter he earned quite a few dollars selling beaver, muskrat, skunk and fox skins to the woolen mill in Spartensburg.

What he made selling skins wasn't nearly enough to pay for all the things Lefty needed, as he put it, to live in the manner in which he'd become accustomed. To do that he also earned money by doing odd jobs around town: chopping firewood, shoveling snow, mowing lawns, painting roofs, digging ditches, whatever. Even in those hard days, Lefty never had trouble getting work, on account of whatever he did was done faster and cheaper than anybody else. Except for hanging wallpaper! When it came to that he may have done it cheaper, but wasn't nearly as good or as fast as Mr. Hutter from up on the Blue Eye road. Aunt Martha learned this the hard way when she hired Lefty to paper her dining room. Ma told her she should have known better than hire a one-armed paper hanger.

The surprising thing about Lefty was he only had one arm . . . . the right one. The left one he'd lost years before he migrated to Spring Creek when (a) a rattlesnake bit his hand and his arm turned to gangrene; or (b) as a young hired man on a farm near East Branch Lefty had to dive through a window when the farmer caught him having a time with the farmer's daughter. (These were the most believable of the stories Lefty told about how it had happened.) It was because Lefty with one arm could do almost anything better than any two-armed man could that he was so much admired by Spring Creekers. Also because of the time Lefty single-handedly kept the wrong man from getting elected to the U.S. Senate in Washington.

Almost everybody who hunted and fished around the Spring Creek area, even the rich Cleveland doctors, knew where they wanted to go, how to get there, and how to return. That's not quite the way it was with the hunting and fishing politicians staying at the Henry place. As often as not they couldn't find their way to where they wanted to go, and if they did, they often as not couldn't find their way back. (LR said this was to be expected considering they were politicians.) For this reason the politicians sometimes hired Lefty as a hunting or fishing guide, and, except for deer hunting, which dogs aren't allowed to do, Adolph went along.

Lefty had taught Adolph two good tricks, one being to fetch a bottle of beer from one of the baskets down in Morton Pond. The other trick was even better than that. When Lefty said, "Heil Hitler," Adolph stood on his hind legs, held one paw straight in front of him and growled while he strutted around in a circle. One time one of the politicians, a Republican, who saw Adolph do that trick was running for U.S. Senator. Immediately he wanted to buy Adolph from Lefty for two hundred dollars, telling the other politicians he could ride a dog like that all the way to Washington. Lefty told the politicians he wouldn't

66

sell Adolph for that or any amount of money. Then the politician tried renting Adolph for a few months for the same amount, and again Lefty turned him down saying it would be wrong for Adolph to get involved in politics for even a short time.

Without Adolph to ride on, the politician didn't get to Washington when the election was held that November. LR, however, wasn't a bit sorry about it, even if the politician was the Republican candidate. The thing was, that particular politician had been a Methodist minister before he'd fallen into politics which meant he didn't smoke, drink or tell lies. LR said there were several good senators in Washington who didn't smoke or drink, but you couldn't be a good senator if you didn't tell lies once in awhile!

# Fourteen
## Preacher Bentley and Apostle Paul Prevent the End of the World

Christmas Morning, Easter Sunday and sometimes on Mother's Day, Spring Creekers filled the pews of the Congregational Church, but that's not the way it was on other Sundays. It bothered the church deacons that even on warm and sunny Sundays when bad weather wasn't an excuse, only thirty to forty regulars would show up. Which included the preacher's wife and the six people in the choir. Even fewer went to the Wednesday evening service since the choir didn't sing and some of the old folks were already in bed.

Some Spring Creekers had good excuses for not going. Aunt Hat was Catholic so she wasn't allowed, and Uncle Glen wouldn't go by himself. On Sunday mornings in winter LR cleaned the store, and he played golf in summer. LR said when he was on a golf course he was closer to God anyway. Mr. Bates and Uncle Mac didn't hear well so for them going to church was a waste of time. Mr. Eddy's excuse was if he went inside the church the foundation would crack. However, the rest of the grown folks in town, numbering about seventy-five, were just plain backsliders because they didn't go to church for no good reason!

One of the things Ma and the other church deacons were supposed to do was go after backsliders. This was important because the deacons all knew very well the people who weren't going to church were the very ones who needed to the most of all. It wasn't that backsliders were bad people, most of them, anyway; it's just that if they would go to church they'd certainly become better people. Another important thing was if more people went to church the collection might be enough for the deacons to pay Pastor Garner a living wage.

I knew about this because once a month the deacons met in our living room and sometimes I'd play in the dining room just across the hall to hear what the deacons had to say. At one of those meetings each deacon was supposed to come up with an idea which might get the backsliders to change their ways. Mrs. Frank, who had been a Catholic, or maybe a Baptist, before she moved to Spring Creek, said maybe they could have a drawing for a prize at each service. Preacher Garner thought if the deacon ladies would make coffee and doughnuts to serve free each Sunday before church that might be just the ticket. Mrs. Maxwell said putting pads on the pews would certainly help. Ma proposed having "missionaries" go around town every Saturday to remind people about there being a church service the next day.

Finally grumpy old Mr. Wagner said what they should do was throw a good scare into everybody. Make those folks realize once and for all "if they weren't church goers they'd fer sure be Hell goers." He said that's how evangelist Preacher Bentley over in Corry put it, and he was packing people by the hundreds into his revival tent every night Thursday through Sunday. They had to use shoe boxes to collect all the money, Mr. Wagner told the deacons, and he knew this for a fact because Mrs. Wagner and he had gone to one of those meetings last Friday night.

At first the deacons didn't think much about letting a revival preacher into the Congregational Church. Mr. Bates claimed all they knew was hellfire and damnation, and Ma said you shouldn't have to scare people into going to church. Mrs. Maxwell had heard a lot of those traveling preachers were just plain crooks out to get folks' hard earned money or relief checks. Mrs. Frank believed that Catholics were excommunicated if they attended a revival meeting.

But old Mr. Wagner said all that was balderdash. He had no doubt whatsoever but what some good old time Hellfire religion was just what the Spring Creek backsliders needed. Mrs. Maxwell said she agreed with Mr. Wagner, but that didn't change her mind about getting pads on the pews. When old Mr. Wagner reminded the other deacons about the shoe boxes full of money, the tide turned. The vote was four to two in favor of getting a revival preacher to have two meetings at the Spring Creek Congregational Church.

Old Mr. Wagner was elected to attend another of Preacher Bentley's revival meetings in Corry to see if he would take on the job for twenty dollars and half of what was collected. Preacher Bentley not only agreed to the offer, as long as he got to divide the money, he said he'd also provide an organist and two singers dressed like angels.

The very next Sunday some of the older Sunday School kids were put to work making signs and posters about Preacher Bentley coming to Spring Creek on Tuesday and Wednesday nights the week after next. The deacons put the signs around town where everybody would see them; in the store window, on the wall of the post office in the store, outside the community building, down at the feedmill and blacksmith shop, and in Miss Jackson's ice cream parlor. Preacher Bentley himself drove down from Corry in his green Packard and nailed big red signs onto telephone poles. The signs warned Spring Creekers that "Judgment Day was Imminent!" If we wanted to go to heaven we'd better go hear him tell about how to do it.

I have to admit I became very concerned about the imminence of the end of the world. M. and H. (sisters) claimed they were happy about the possibility since they would go up to Heaven with Ma and LR while I'd go down to the other place where I belonged. LR said the end of the world was the best thing that could happen considering Roosevelt was president. Ma told me to pay no attention to what M. and H. had said because I'd get to Heaven just as fast as they did. Besides that, she said it wasn't true the world was going to end any time soon anyway. That was just Preacher Bentley's way of getting folks to come hear him preach.

Tuesday night Ma took me to the revival meeting with her. When we got to the church, a lady in a long blue dress was playing the pump organ instead of Mrs. Garner. Up on the stage a skinny man with gray hair and a gray beard was sitting in one of two rocking chairs. A little ways behind him two blonde girls wearing long white dresses were singing; "The Devil's coming round the mountain; he'll be here any day. Sinners better pay attention to what the preacher has to say." Or something like that. They were older than my sisters and a lot prettier, too.

After the angels sang two more songs, which weren't at all like the ones in the church's hymn book, the skinny man, who turned out to be Preacher Bentley, stood up and told everybody to join him and the angels in singing Hymn 207, "When the role Is Called Up Yonder." While they were singing I looked over the crowd to see how many backsliders had come. Not many! In fact, the church was less than half full, and most of the folks were Sunday regulars who had come just because they were curious. The only backsliders there were Mr. and Mrs. Bailey and their boy, Beany, who was in my class but two years older; Mrs. Perkins and her deaf and dumb sister, Alma; Hawker's Ma and Pa; and the Jasper family from up on Blue Eye Hill. There were also five people I didn't recognize.

After the second hymn Preacher Bentley said the lady playing the organ was "his Heaven-sent little woman," and the two singing angels were their "Heaven-sent daughters." It seemed that for twenty dollars and half the collection the deacons had gotten a good bargain: a preacher who knew about the Day of Judgment coming, a Heaven-sent organist who played better than Mrs. Garner, and two Heaven-sent good-looking girls who sang like angels.

Preacher Bentley began preaching, walking back and forth across the stage talking in a low voice which made everybody listen carefully. Little by little his voice got louder and louder and he paced back and forth faster and faster. By the time he got to the part where he told us all what miserable sinners we all were, he was shouting, and watching him made everybody's head turn back and forth at a great rate. All of a sudden he stopped in mid-pace, jumped off the stage and began pointing at different people. He told them they had better repent and change their ways or what was going to happen to them was so bad he didn't want to scare people by talking about it. But he did anyway. They were going to be "roasted alive in the devil's fiery ovens for all eternity and the ovens were mighty hot and eternity was a mighty long time." Then he yelled at all of us, "And don't think for a minute there won't be room for you because Hell is a mighty big place! Bigger than Texas! Bigger than the whole United States. Oh yes, there's plenty of room down there for everybody, and don't you ever forget that!"

Mr. Johanson was one of the men Reverend Bentley had pointed at and advised to change his ways or else. Everybody knew Mr. Johanson was the most religious man in all of Spring Creek. He didn't smoke, drink, chew tobacco, spit, or swear. He went to church every Sunday and Wednesday night and always sat in the front. He was a church usher, and would drive his Model A when folks needed a ride to funerals out at the cemetery. In addition to all that, Mrs. Johanson was a church deacon, and when the collection plate was passed, both of them put money in; not just one of them like it was with most families. Now, if Mr. Johanson couldn't make it to Heaven the way he was, then nobody else in Spring Creek or even Spring Creek Township, had any chance whatsoever!

Preacher Bentley hopped back up on the stage and leaned on the podium. His voice dropped to a loud whisper, like he was telling an important secret. He said he was going to tell us a guaranteed foolproof way to keep out of the Devil's hot hands. His voice got louder again as he advised us to listen close because what he was going to tell us was the most important thing we'd ever hear. And we'd better hear it good; our days were clearly numbered.

Suddenly he whacked the podium with his Bible, shouting that Armageddon, whatever that was, and the Day of Judgment and the end of the world were all so close you could smell the fire and the brimstone and the burning of flesh! It was so close you could even *see* it. The signs were everywhere if you knew what to look for. "Floods, famines, pestilence, earthquakes, droughts and the other terrible signs of the coming of Judgment Day are happening all over the world and right on schedule," is what Preacher Bentley hollered. "Only two weeks ago right here in Spring Creek the sun turned black in the middle of the Day of Reckoning, but being sinners you didn't know it was a sign!" (Preacher Bentley must not have read the Corry paper the day after it happened. It said the sun was blocked out by clouds of dust blown all the way up from Oklahoma.) Then he held up his Bible saying, "It's all spelled out in plain English right here in the Book of Revelations, and if you'd read the Bible you'd know what I'm saying is the 'Deeevine' truth!"

Preacher Bentley started reading from Revelations about great earthquakes, burning mountains, plagues, famines and all the things that were signs of the beginning of the end. Lightning, falling stars, and *fiery lights in the sky* were other things to watch for. He shouted, "These things are happening just as St. John said they would when the Day of Judgment was approaching and now what are you sinners going to do about it?"

Reverend Bentley went on about what it was us sinners had to do to be saved. In front of everybody we were supposed to say loud and clear we were sinners and were very sorry about it and we wouldn't sin anymore. Once we had done that he was authorized to save our miserable souls from the horned monster. He pointed at himself and shouted so loudly they could probably hear it all the way down to the store, "I am your ticket to Heaven and your passport to the Promised Land!" He said right now, this very night, people could show they meant business about wanting to walk up those golden stairs to Heaven instead of sliding down that coal chute to Hell.

Right when he said that the two girls said "Hallelujah" two times and Mrs. Bentley began playing the organ while the two girls passed the collection plates. While the plates were being passed Preacher Bentley said that everybody who wanted to deny the Devil his chance at them should march right up on the stage and get saved . . . after they'd had a chance to put something in the plate. "Do it tonight, because the world is playing its last inning," he whispered.

After that you can just bet I slid off the seat so I could march right up and get saved, but Ma grabbed my arm and told me to stay put. She whispered we didn't have to worry about getting saved because it wasn't really necessary no matter what Preacher Bentley said. And I shouldn't worry about Judgment Day being just about here, because Preacher Bentley had absolutely no way of knowing that, no matter what he said. All the regular churchgoers must have felt the same as Ma because not one of them took Preacher Bentley up on his offer to save them.

Five people marched to the front of the church, but not one was a Spring Creek backslider. They were the five people nobody recognized, and they all seemed to know just how to go about getting saved. Preacher Bentley didn't even have to tell them to stand in a circle and join hands with Preacher Bentley and the two angels. Then he went into a long prayer which he ended by telling the recording angel up in Heaven to make sure he wrote the names of these five people in Heaven's Book of Reservations. He didn't say anything about any of the rest of us getting reservations, especially after he'd glanced over at the collection plates.

Then Preacher Bentley slowly lowered himself into his rocking chair, and in a wavering voice announced he felt terrible. He'd been sent to save all the Spring Creek sinners and he'd only saved five. He had failed us, and it was his fault that each one of us was going to suffer terrible pain and anguish, which is something he'd never be able to forget. After saying that, he took out a handkerchief, gave his eyes a wipe, and stepped back to the podium.

In a strong voice he told everybody to come back the next night for a final chance at keeping out of the fiery pit and walking through the Pearly Gate. He said for that meeting he'd invited a very important visitor who should do a better job than he had to save us all from eternal damnation. He pointed at the second rocker on the stage and said right there in that chair Apostle Paul is going to sit because he's making a special trip down from Heaven to be with the people of Spring Creek. He knows Spring Creekers are good people but he also knows they don't read the Bible, or go to church or appreciate about getting saved. After that announcement, Preacher Bentley prayed for awhile, Mrs. Bentley played the organ, and everybody headed for home.

All in all, the Tuesday night revival meeting hadn't been much of a success. Not many backsliders had even bothered to go, and of those who did none had been saved. As for the five people who did, Mr. Wagner was pretty sure he'd seen the same ones get saved up in Corry, too. After splitting the collection with Preacher Bentley all that was left for the deacons was fourteen dollars and twenty-five cents. Preacher Bentley told Mr. Wagner before he left he was wastin' his valuable time in Spring Creek, and if he hadn't already spent the twenty dollars he wouldn't come back the next night and be bringing Apostle Paul.

Well, it was a good thing he had spent the twenty dollars, and even a better thing that he had signed up Apostle Paul to help out at the Wednesday night meeting. After supper Wednesday evening just as it was getting dark, something happened which got almost every Spring Creeker who could walk to go to Preacher Bentley's second revival meeting. Backsliders were there, and sinners, regular church goers, and farm folks from out in the township. Plus quite a few people who'd never ever been in a church before. All the pews were jam packed, and folks were standing up in back and out in the vestibule where they couldn't even see Preacher Bentley or the Angels up on the stage.

The reason for this was the sign that appeared in the sky, the fiery lights which Preacher Bentley had said the night before foretold the end of the world! Strange fiery lights the likes of which no one had ever seen before. Or maybe since.

Ma wasn't planning to take me with her to the Wednesday night meeting, so Grampa Charley and I were playing cribbage while she got ready to go. A little after seven o'clock, about an hour before the revival meeting was to begin, Ern, the big boy from next door, banged on our window and motioned for us to come outside to look at the sky. We hurried out and what we saw looked like Fourth of July fireworks except there was no noise. Streaks of bright yellow, red and green light flashed across the sky, some dying out and some ending in big swirls. Purple lights and green stripes flashed and now and then a colored ball would spin for awhile and fly apart. Fiery lights in the sky!

I may not have mentioned before that Ma had been a school teacher before my two older sisters were born. (They turned out to be more than a full-time job so she had to quit.) Having been a school teacher she knew about a lot of things, and she said what we were seeing was a very unusual display of the aurora borealis. (Which means northern lights.) At certain times of the year, northern lights could be seen over Spring Creek, but they always appeared like flimsy-colored sheets flapping in the wind, not at all like fireworks. I had to decide was Ma right or was she just saying that so I'd stop being scared?

76

Down near the store several people were standing in the middle of the Corry to Garland road looking at the sky. The number grew as more curious and/or apprehensive Spring Creekers joined them. Including Ern and me. Inasmuch as a few people in the crowd had heard Preacher Bentley's warning about fiery lights in the sky the night before, the news about the imminence of Judgment Day was spreading fast.

Nobody, not even old folks, had ever seen anything like it. When I told Mr. Washburn, who had probably never been to church in his life, that Ma had said they were just northern lights, he grumbled, "I'll tell you sonny; I've seen northern lights before and those ain't no Goddamned northern lights at all!" About that time church deacon Mr. Wagner and Pastor Garner walked by on their way to the revival meeting. Several of the folks asked if the fiery lights in the sky were the sign Preacher Bentley had warned about. Mr. Wagner said it might be a good idea if everybody came along to the church to see what Preacher Bentley and Apostle Paul did have to say about them.

At that moment, the church bell began to toll like it did when there was a funeral. Preacher Bentley had told old Bob, the bell ringer, to ring it that way. That started the march up to the church, and I again tagged after Ern, because maybe Ma hadn't been right about them being the northern lights after all.

Ern and I got there in time to squeeze into the very last pew on the right. Ern sat next to the aisle and I was squeezed against Muley Richard's Ma. Like the night before, Mrs. Bentley was at the organ and the two angels were singing, but this time, Preacher Bentley was sitting in his rocker talking to the other rocking chair. It was rocking back and forth although it didn't seem as if anybody was in it. Pretty soon he got up and walked slowly to the podium, but instead of having everybody sing a hymn like the night before, Preacher Bentley got right into it. After telling us again that the organ player and the singing angels were Heaven-sent, he introduced Apostle Paul who was rocking away in the seemingly empty rocking chair. Like the lights in the sky, the way that empty chair rocked back and forth was very mysterious.

Probably because the church was stuffed with people and maybe because he wanted to impress Apostle Paul, Preacher

78

Bentley didn't start off soft and slow like he had the night before. Right off the bat he banged the pulpit with his Bible, glared at everybody and said in a loud, deep voice, "The Terrible Day of Atonement is upon thee and me! Armageddon is upon us and at this very minute that terrible war is being fought in the sky. Right over this very church!" He went on to say that time had all but run out for us wretched Spring Creek sinners. He shouted about how he pitied the people who'd been at the revival the night before and hadn't been saved because it might be too Late. He truly and sincerely hoped that was not to be the case. If it was, then he was to blame for the fact that our poor souls would roast in Hell's hot ovens for all eternity and then some!

After that Preacher Bentley turned the meeting over to Apostle Paul. He said, for the benefit of the sinners in the audience who wouldn't be able to actually see or hear Apostle Paul, that he would repeat Apostle Paul's words for us. First off Apostle Paul announced, through Preacher Bentley, that if Judgment Day wasn't upon the earth, he, Apostle Paul, wouldn't have bothered to come to this meeting. People who didn't believe it was here should walk out of the church and look at the sky. If they still didn't think so, they might as well keep right on walking back to their houses, get in their beds, pull their covers over their heads and wait for the Devil to come by, grab 'em by their arms and legs and drag 'em down to his place. Then Apostle Paul explained that in this crisis, he'd been charged with helping Preacher Bentley save as many wretched souls as possible before the fateful day of reckoning which could be as soon as tomorrow but no later than Saturday afternoon. We'd know which day when we were awakened by Gabriel's horn and the crashing of thunders. This was our final chance to be saved, and we'd all better get right to it before it was too late.

Mrs. Bentley pumped the organ, again playing, "We Shall Come Rejoicing," and the two angel girls walked up the aisles each carrying a big red and white shoe box for people to put money in. It occurred to me at that minute that Ma had been right all along! If it really was the end of the world, why would they bother taking up a collection? Strangely enough, not many other people seemed to have thought about that. When the angel girls got to where we were in the back of the church, the boxes were jammed clear full of money, and it wasn't only coins and one-dollar bills either. (Just like Mr. Wagner said was the way it had been in Corry.) Ern, who made money cutting lawns in summer and shoveling snow the rest of the year, put in all he had with him, four one-dollar bills and three nickels. When he did, the pretty angel in charge of the shoebox, winked at him! Muley's Ma was on relief but she also put in all she had, a dollar and twenty-seven cents.

When the angles got their boxes of money back to the front of the church, Mrs. Bentley played the organ especially loud and Preacher Bentley said for all the sinners, who were going to answer Apostle Paul's call to stand up and raise both hands over their heads. Well, more than half of the crowd did just that, which made Preacher Bentley raise his own arms and say, "Praise the Lord; they have seen the light!" (Probably meaning the lights in the sky.)

He picked up Apostle Paul in his rocker and set him at the front of one of the two aisles leading to the front of the church. (After he sat it down, the chair continued to rock back and forth.) Then he stood in front of the other aisle and told all the people who were going to be saved that they should form lines down the two aisles. As soon as they'd made it up to the front, each one had to had to get down on their knees and say they were a sinner who'd seen the light and wanted to be saved from eternal damnation.

First in Apostle Paul's line were backsliders, Mr. and Mrs. Mailer, and all seven of the Mailer kids. Except for the annual Christmas plays when everybody got free candy, not one of 'em ever came to church. Or even Sunday School! Right behind them were two more backsliders, Clifford and Lefty, the town's foremost bachelors and drinkin' buddies. Neither of them had been to church since anybody could remember. Then there was the Barnhart family who lived on a farm a ways out of town and only came to church on Easter Sunday. Following them was B.O. Barton, who everybody knew always had a pint of something in his back pocket. After him thirty or more sinners were lined up, including quite a few regular churchgoers, and Hawker and Weiner who both went to Sunday School.

Heading the line of sinners in Preacher Bentley's aisle were two backsliders, Bucky Sellers and "Cupey" Dahl. I knew from what people said that they were living together in sin, but I didn't know just what that sin was. Behind them was Clem, who wasn't married but was always having babies anyway. Then it was the Skinner brothers, who'd been in jail for selling moonshine, and after them, another thirty or so more people, including Ern. I don't think Ern was as much interested in getting saved as he was getting another close look at the angel who'd winked at him.

All the time people were shuffling down the aisles Mrs. Bentley played the organ. When everybody's finally had their turn to be saved, Preacher Bentley stood next to Apostle Paul's chair, clapped his hands, did a little dance with his feet and said how happy he and Apostle Paul were they'd rescued so many Spring Creekers from the clutches of the devil. Then he made what he called "a miraculous announcement," one which he said was bound to make both the saved and the sinners all as happy as he was. He said that before the service Apostle Paul had talked at length with whoever was in charge of ending the world, telling him or her, such as the case may be, that he and Preacher Bentley needed more time, to save all the people who needed saving. Well, during the saving that very evening Apostle Paul had been notified his request had been granted. "Praise be," Preacher Bentley shouted, "all you Spring Creek people who haven't been saved still have time!"

Then he reminded everybody about his revival meetings in Corry every Thursday, Friday, Saturday, and Sunday night where they could still come and get saved. Following that, he thanked the Lord for all that had happened that night in Spring Creek. I suppose that included the fiery lights in the sky and the full shoe boxes. He reminded the recording angel in Heaven to make sure all the names of the saved that night would get into the Book of Reservations, then turned to Apostle Paul's rocker to say how much he appreciated his help and told him to come again as soon as he could manage it. At that very moment the chair stopped rocking!

After one stanza of "We Shall Come Rejoicing," the meeting was over and I walked home with Ma. The lights in the sky had gone away leaving only the stars and a half moon which all looked very natural. I told her how I'd figured out she was right about them being the northern lights because if it was really going to be the end of the world Preacher Bentley wouldn't have sent the collection boxes around. When we got home she told LR about the meeting. He said he'd wished he'd been there to see Clifford and Lefty talk to an empty chair. LR also told Ma that he was glad Judgment Day had been postponed because now people who were no longer sinners might pay their store bills.

The next day Ma and the deacons met at our house after supper and agreed that having a revival preacher may have been a mistake but a good one. Half of the collection taken on the second night amounted to $332.30, which is more than was usually collected in a whole month of Sundays. The *Corry Evening Journal* had an article about the unusual show the northern lights had put on for people in the northeast on Tuesday evening. No mention was made about Armageddon or anything like that, although the article did state a few people had believed it meant the world was coming to an end. If the reporter had been in Spring Creek Wednesday night he would have known it was more than a few!

By the third Sunday after Preacher Bentley and Apostle Paul's meeting, most everyone saved had pretty much gone back to their sinful ways and the backsliders were backsliding again. Before they'd even settled their store bills. Oh yes, and Ern never quite got over having given away all his money. Still, when you stop and think about it, four dollars and fifteen cents isn't much to pay to have an angel wink at you.

# Fifteen
## Why Ma Left Home

The store was closed every Wednesday afternoon and sometimes during the summer we'd go on a picnic over by Goose Creek on the Loomis farm. To get to the picnic place you drove through Mr. Loomis's gate and followed two ruts through a cow pasture for about a half mile to a flat grassy place with trees and cow flops all around. This was on a bank about eight feet above Goose Creek, a wide, fairly shallow, gravel-bottomed stream meandering through the pasture. Most times when we went there LR parked the Studebaker with the front wheels as close as he could to the edge of the bank. He liked to do this because it scared Ma and me while the girls, M. and H., thought it was funny.

One of those Wednesdays LR was slow to hit the brakes. Both front wheels dropped over the edge of the bank, the bank sort of caved in, and the car rolled down into Goose Creek. Even though Ma knew as well as anybody the creek wasn't more than a foot or so deep, you'd have thought we were all going to drown by the way she screeched. I guess LR was a bit concerned too, because he said, "Horse shit!" and some other bad cuss words.

Ma's shriek and the fact I was afraid of water caused me to get hysterical which in turn made our dog, Rabbit, howl. LR turned off the motor and stepped out into the creek to assess the damages, which were none. I figured, since he very well knew what I thought about water, he'd carry me ashore, but he just told Ma he was going to get Mr. Loomis to bring his horses down and haul the car back up the bank. Taking a couple Fort Pitt beers from the ice chest, he headed back up through the pasture towards Mr. Loomis's house leaving Ma to deal with having to get me back to dry land. The girls and Rabbit were already out wading around looking for crabs.

83

After what seemed a long time Mr. Loomis and LR came back down through the pasture behind two enormous, mean looking, frothy-mouthed horses. It seemed from the way they were walking that they (LR and Mr. Loomis, not the horses) might have been sampling something more than the Fort Pitt beer. Ma pretended not to notice and was real nice to Mr. Loomis so he'd get our car out of Goose Creek.

Mr. Loomis backed the horses to where the car had slid down the bank and tied a big long rope between them and the Studebaker's back bumper. Then he whacked the horses' rumps with the reins and yelled, "Gee-up, God dammit!" at them a couple of times. I'd been worrying about us probably having to leave our car in the creek forever, but I needn't have. Just to show you how big those horses were, they didn't struggle a bit hauling the car out of the water and up the bank. After Mr. Loomis untied the rope, he and LR had a couple more Fort Pitts because of all the work they'd done. The horses, who had really done it, stood there stamping their big feet and looking meaner than ever. Probably they were provoked because LR hadn't offered them beer too.

After a bit LR gave Mr. Loomis some money and Mr. Loomis "Gee-up, God dammited" the horses to get them started back to the barn. They weren't even out of ear shot before Ma, who'd been acting real nice, cut loose on LR saying we couldn't get home fast enough in order for her and me to leave it. This set me to sobbing again which I managed to keep doing most of the way home until Ma had a change of heart and announced since nobody'd drowned she guessed we'd not leave after all. "But," she told me, "we definitely will if your father doesn't change his ways!" He didn't.

What Ma really objected to most about LR was what she claimed was his drinkin' problem, because it was mostly after drinking that he did what Ma considered to be damn fool things. Like driving the car into Goose Creek. He'd always argued he had no problem with drinking, and he didn't see how it had anything to do with what she said were damn fool things which he didn't think were damn fool things in the first place.

LR wasn't an everyday drinker, but on Sunday mornings every couple weeks or so and on holidays when he didn't have to put in twelve hours at the store, he visited the clubs he belonged to up in Corry. The trouble was he belonged to almost every club there was, so by the time he'd made the rounds visiting all his brothers at the Moose, Elks, VFW, Polack, and Italian Clubs it was pretty easy to tell he'd had a few.

Ma, on the other hand, was a teetotaler who didn't belong to clubs and lodges and such where drinking was the main thing to do. The strongest thing she ever drank was Aunt Hat's two-day-old coffee. What Ma belonged to was the Parent-Teachers Association, the Ladies Aid Society, the Bridge Club, and, as I've said before she was a deacon in the Congregational Church. It was on account of her being a deacon that she did finally get so mad at LR she actually did walk out on him, dragging me along.

Reverend Garner, who'd been the pastor at the church since before I could remember, was moving away and a new pastor had come to Spring Creek to take his place. On the afternoon of the Sunday the new preacher took over the pulpit, Ma had arranged for Reverend Garner, the other deacons and the new preacher to meet at our house at three in the afternoon so they could drink tea and talk about church stuff.

This was one of those Sundays LR had visited the clubs. When he got home about two in the afternoon, Ma said he was in no condition to be seen by the new minister or the deacons and she sent him upstairs to sleep it off. At three o'clock the meeting started in the living room, right below the bedroom LR was in.

Everything would probably have gone fine if the new preacher's deep, loud voice hadn't sounded exactly like Uncle Don's! Uncle Don wasn't a real uncle, but, since he owned the One Stop Grocery on East Main in Corry, he and LR were buddies. Drinkin' buddies, that is, and he often accompanied LR on his club tour, as he had done that very morning. The new preacher's loud voice woke up LR, and LR, having forgotten about the deacons' meeting, thought it was Uncle Don down in the living room.

The new preacher's boy was my age, and we were playing on the floor in our dining room just across the front hall from the living room. From where I was I could see the bottom half of the stairs, so when I heard LR start down, I glanced up and saw his bare legs. When the rest of him came into view and I observed he was wearing only his BVD underwear shorts, a necktie, and a lampshade over his head. Also, he was carrying my real-looking toy rifle on his shoulder like he was in a parade.

Because of the lampshade, LR couldn't see there were a bunch of church deacons in the living room. Nor could he see that it wasn't Uncle Don who was doing the loud talking. From beneath the lamp shade LR loudly asked, "Who let that damned old reprobate into our house?"

Ma saw him about then, and right in front of the new preacher she yelled, "Lester; what the hell are you doing?" Even if he wasn't thinking just right, he knew when Ma called him Lester and said a swear word right afterwards, he was in serious trouble—for whatever reason. He immediately did a smart about-face with the gun still on his shoulder and marched back up the stairs without even saying hello to the deacons or getting introduced to the new minister.

It was good Reverend Garner was at that meeting because he'd known LR for a long time, LR didn't go to church much, but he saw to it that the preacher's grocery billy every month was only about half what it was supposed to be. This was because LR knew Spring Creek preachers didn't get paid much, and they sure couldn't count on the collection plates each Sunday. Right after LR's surprise appearance Reverend Garner told the new preacher and the deacons that LR was one of the main reasons he was sorry he was leaving Spring Creek. LR had always been such a good, generous friend, and he was so good at making people laugh and have fun. Reverend Garner said LR's practical jokes kept Spring Creekers on their toes, so I guess he was thinking about the nail-in-the-counter trick.

Ma's face got less red, and the other deacons chimed in about what a good man LR was and said to Ma he must be a joy to live with. She sort of smiled, and then they got back to talking about what they were talking about before LR had appeared.

Ma missed the evening service because she was too busy packing our clothes. My sisters felt bad they had missed seeing what had happened because they were at a friend's house. Nevertheless, they happily pitched right in to help Ma and me get our suitcases loaded. They, of course, were going to stay with LR since he owned the store and the Studabaker.

This time no amount of whining and sobbing on my part made Ma change her mind, and before long we had checked out of our house and into Uncle Mac and Aunt Mildred's across the street. In the morning Uncle Mac was going to take us to Ma's cousin's place up in Corry where I guess we were going to live.

About nine o'clock that night just as Ma was sending me up to bed in the guest room, there was a commotion on Uncle Mac's front porch. LR had rounded up Uncle Glen, Aunt Hat, Aunt Martha, Aunt Donna, Uncle Lon, Reverend Garner, Grampa Charlie, Clifford, and Mrs. Brundage, and they were all waiting out there to talk Ma out of leaving town. Ma went out onto the porch, and LR made a good and sincere-sounding political speech about how sorry he was he'd embarrassed her like he did. Then, right there with Reverend Garner and all the others as his witnesses, LR swore if she promised not to leave, he would never embarrass her like that again. Ever!

After listening to LR's speech and the comments of her neighbors and relatives, Ma finally said all right, we'd go back home. She warned LR, however, that if he ever went back on his vow not to repeat his bad behaviors, we'd leave again and never, under any circumstances would we return home again.

Well, would you believe LR actually kept his promise? It's true! Never again did LR come downstairs to a deacons' meeting in his BVD underpants, a tie, and a lampshade.

# Sixteen
## Orry's Place

Ma was the church deacon, but it was LR who did the most to help out poor people, and due to the Great Depression there was no shortage of poor people in Spring Creek Township. For example there was Preacher Garner, whose family was especially bad off since Spring Creek preachers were poor even when there wasn't a Great Depression. LR charged Mrs. Garner only half price for what she bought at the store, then at the end of the month when she came in to pay up he marked the bill down 20% because her husband was in the ministry.

And then there was Mrs. Woodrow, whose husband (Mr. Woodrow) had gone to an early grave during the great flu epidemic of 1919. Mrs. Woodrow could most likely have gotten by with her relief check and food stamps if she hadn't had to support Clem, her grown-up daughter. Clem didn't have much going on in the brain department, and she didn't have much in the way of a husband either. What she did have was five kids, ages two to six, and no idea in the world who their Pas were. Every Friday morning Mrs. Woodrow walked to the store with one or two of Clem's older kids to get their week's supply of groceries. Her shopping list never varied so LR didn't even have to look at it to know she wanted five pounds of flour, two pounds of sugar, four pounds of dried beans, a gallon of fresh milk and six cans of condensed, a peck of potatoes, two pounds of lard, a box of Mother's Oats and three pounds of sliced baloney. That was all she could afford, but every week LR saw to it she took home some apples, canned vegetables, wieners, soup bones, bread, ginger snaps, Ovaltine and a bag of penny candy.

There was also a bag of penny candy in each of the large cardboard boxes of groceries LR delivered free of charge every

Thanksgiving and Christmas to the Township's ten or twelve poorest farm families. These families worked hard to make ends meet but one thing or another—poor soil, lousy weather, bad health or just plain rotten luck, always kept the ends a long ways apart. Almost every nickel they got from the milk plant each month went for things they couldn't eat, grain and udder balm for cows, kerosene for lanterns, horse linament for horses, cough syrup for kids, and tar paper for roofs and walls, and like that.

All the people LR helped were very thankful for what he did and let him know how they felt, as best they could. That was why quite a few babies who arrived in Spring Creek Township during those years got to be named Leslie. Even Clem named her last one Leslie, which, for some reason, didn't please Ma a bit. As for folks who weren't having babies, they gave LR presents of whatever they had any of to give away, things like wild strawberry jam, honey, maple syrup, walnuts, and apples. Then there was Orry who showed his appreciation the most of all.

Orry lived in a cabin on the left side of the road half-way between Spring Creek and Garland, not far from where he had once had a sawmill. When the big trees were all gone, Orry closed the mill and used leftover boards to construct the cabin, a shed for the big red gasoline-powered generator he'd used to run the sawmill, a comfortable backhouse, and a long low building with a dirt floor.

That building was next to a small stream on the other side of a clearing in the woods below Orry's cabin. It was where he kept his "critters," wild animals and birds, in chicken wire cages. His collection of critters had started with a skunk family he'd removed from their place of residence beneath his cabin. Shortly thereafter, Orry captured a porcupine which had strolled into the generator building, and about the same time he found a half-starved red fox puppy lying next to the backhouse. That's when he got the idea for a wild animal zoo which he could charge people to visit and make a good living.

Before long Orry's zoo featured, in addition to the skunks, a fox, and a porcupine, two raccoons, three gray squirrels, two groundhogs, some rabbits, three possums, two barn owls, a buzzard, and several pheasants. At the rear of the building was a fenced area in which he kept a small four-point buck, a lady goat to keep the buck company, two sheep, and two geese. Near the front door a crow was attached to a perch by a leather thong. Orry claimed he'd taught the crow to talk, but nobody ever heard it say anything except "sunnabitch" which it squawked whenever anyone walked through the door.

The trouble was not many people walked through the door since everybody living in Spring Creek Township could see wild animals just by looking out their kitchen window. At the same time, not many people from Corry, Youngsville, or any other big city went past Orry's place because in those days not many city folks drove on the dirt road from Corry to Garland. With hardly any paying customers and having so many mouths to feed, Orry was soon flat broke. LR found that out the day Orry walked the three miles to the store to ask for spoiled fruit and vegetables, stale bread, meat scraps and anything else which he could feed to the animals. Afterward, LR saw to it Orry got his weekly supply of garbage for the animals plus things for Orry himself to eat, and gasoline to run the generator.

Sometimes when LR took Orry his weekly rations of food and garbage I'd ride along, and while the two of them sat at the kitchen table having a glass of Four Roses, I was allowed to take some garbage down to feed the animals. The last time I did that was when I discovered skunks can stand up on their front legs. I also learned that's something they sometimes do when they're planning to spray somebody. It's not that I couldn't read Orry's hand lettered sign, *BEWAR!! Skunks Are Loded.* on the front of the skunk family's cage. Furthermore, I knew it meant the skunks had not been de-scented, so if you touched or poked one it could make you very sorry you did. Therefore I had no excuse for giving one of the smaller skunks a very gentle prod with the handle of the broom which leaned against their cage.

I'm not going to go into all the details about the way I stood there marveling at how a skunk could stand on its front legs, thereby providing it with a stationary, easy to hit target. Nor am I going to say much about what happened afterward: the standing undressed in the cold creek while LR scrubbed me with a brush and Fels Naptha soap; or watching Orry bury my clothes and sneakers in a deep hole near the edge of the woods; or the second scrubbing Ma gave me when I got home, using Lifebuoy soap, baking soda and hot water. But I will tell you when you're on the receiving end of whatever it is a skunk sprays you with, you know you've been hit with something bad. The smell is so powerful you can hardly breathe or even see, for that matter. I personally guarantee it's an event you'll remember for a long time.

For more than two years LR saw to it that Orry and the animals ate properly. Then one Sunday morning in March when LR made a delivery to Orry, he discovered Orry had passed away in his cot during the night. Using the nearest telephone, which was back at the store, he reported what he'd found to the Warren County Sheriff's department, and the coroner who met LR at Orry's place said it looked to him like Orry had died of plain old age.

Since Orry had no relatives, or at least none he wanted to talk about, LR arranged for Orry's funeral and reserved him a place in the Garland cemetery. Also, because Orry's place was in Spring Creek Township and LR was a township supervisor, he had Clifford, the Spring Creek Township employee, make a trip to Orry's every day with the Township dump truck to look after the critters.

Not many people were at the cemetery the rainy Wednesday afternoon Orry was buried. Of course LR and Ma were there, and the Tripp family who lived not far from Orry's, a couple old-timers who'd worked at Orry's sawmill, the minister from the Garland church, and Old Judge Mosher. Because of the rain, or maybe because he didn't have a lot to say about Orry, the minister consigned Orry to his allotted place in the cemetery in short order. Afterward Old Judge Mosher caught up with LR and Ma as they walked back to LR's Studebaker.

Some years before Old Judge Mosher had been a lawyer down in Youngstown, Ohio. Every spring and fall, regular as a clock, he drove all the way to Warren County to hunt and fish, always booking at the Garland Inn. He probably wasn't married, or if he was, he didn't want to be, because one spring he never checked out and had lived at the Inn every since. Old Judge

Mosher didn't practice law any more, but local folks sometimes went to him for a little legal advice. Orry had done just that, asking for help in making a will. That was why Old Judge Mosher wanted to talk to Ma and LR; Orry had left everything he owned, lock, stock and barrel, to LR.

Back in the saloon at the Garland Inn Old Judge Mosher had Stumps, the saloon's famous no-hands bartender, get the will and a letter addressed to LR from the safe under the bar. In the letter Orry said when he passed on, which he calculated could happen any time, he was leaving what he owned to LR. He figured LR had it coming in payment for all LR had given to him, and he didn't want to leave this world beholden to nobody!

With Stumps as a witness, Old Judge Mosher read the hand-written, four-sentence will. Sentence one repeated what Orry had said in the letter; all of his property was to be deeded to LR. Sentence two instructed LR to free all the birds and animals except the goat, the turkey and the sheep. Sentence three said LR should sell them and use the money to pay the undertaker, and maybe buy a small headstone with "Orry" on it. The last sentence told LR to buy himself a fifth of Four Roses with the money left over. (There wasn't but he did anyway, in memory of good old Orry.)

A few months after inheriting Orry's place, LR leased the building where Orry had kept the critters to a local gunsmith, thinking he was going to use it as a place to fix and sell guns. Before long the gunsmith had removed the wire cages, put in a cement floor and relocated the doors so it faced the Corry—Garland road. He put a wooden counter across one end of the building and built a large stone fireplace at the other. Out back at the edge of the woods and on the other side of a small bridge over the stream, he built two outhouses, one for "bucks", the other for "does." Next he had some old tree stumps bulldozed away to make a parking area, bought a bunch of tables and chairs, and finally nailed up a big sign saying, DEERHEAD INN: COLD BEER AND COCKTAILS.

LR was surprised but not upset that the gunsmith had converted the critter building into a saloon instead of a gun shop. After all, LR had nothing against saloons. Ma, on the other hand did, and she was very upset because in her opinion it wasn't at all fitting for a church deacon's husband to own a building where alcoholic beverages were sold. She informed LR in no uncertain terms he had to cancel the gunsmith's lease and close the saloon, but LR said that wouldn't be legal since the lease didn't say anything about the building not being made into a saloon. Five weeks later things went Ma's way anyway when the state police legally did shut down the Deerhead Inn.

The first week the saloon was open very few customers showed up for the cold beer or cocktails. During the second week business began to pick up considerably after the gunsmith had the (rumor had it) Mafia-owned Erie County Pin Ball Machine Company in Corry install a bunch of one-armed bandits. (Slot machines.) During the third and fourth weeks the Deerhead was a very busy place every day of the week, Sundays included. This was rather surprising, considering nobody living in or around Spring Creek was supposed to have much money to spend, and even less to throw away.

The news about the slot machines had spread fast and far, so it wasn't poor Spring Creekers who were drinking and pulling the handles on the slot machines, but folks from Youngsville, Corry, Pittsfield, Grand Valley, Spartensburg and even Warren. Since they all had to drive their cars to get to the Deerhead, the parking lot was usually full to the brim, just as it was the Sunday afternoon the state police from the Warren barracks arrived in two police cars and a Warren county utility truck. After telling the customers to be on their way, the police loaded the slot machines into the truck and the gunsmith into one of the police cars. They then headed back to Warren where the courthouse and jail was. The slot machines were put in the basement of the courthouse and the gunsmith put in the jail because only the Elks, the Veterans, Odd Fellows, and clubs like that were allowed to have slot machines and sell alcoholic beverages on Sundays.

LR decided he'd just as soon not be a land baron, especially one owning a saloon of ill repute. That's why he sold Orry's place dirt cheap to the first person who wanted to buy it, Paddy from Pittsburgh. For several years Paddy had paid Orry a few dollars each summer so he and his family could pitch their tent for a few weeks down in the flats beside the stream. When he heard about the Deerhead Inn being shut down by the police, Paddy decided if LR would sell Orry's place to him he'd quit his steel mill job, move his family from the city into the woods, and turn the Deerhead into a legitimate bar and restaurant.

It wasn't long before Paddy did just that. By operating in accordance with the law and catering to the desire of hunters and fishermen for a well-stocked bar, a great ham sandwich, pickled eggs and a warm fireplace, Paddy's Deerhead Inn soon began to turn a good profit even without slot machines.

## Postscript to Chapter Sixteen

After World War II, Paddy turned the Deerhead over to his son who had put off a very promising art career to serve in the Air Force. In a short time the son and his wife had enlarged the building to accommodate more people and expanded the kitchen in order to offer a menu of considerably more than ham sandwiches and pickled eggs. They didn't alter the Deerhead's naturally rustic interior; however they did install indoor plumbing and cover the walls with a number of the son's works of art.

Excellent meals were served, which, along with the ambiance of the Inn, and the display of so many superb paintings, resulted in the Deerhead Inn becoming the favorite restaurant of an ever-increasing number of people from near and far, despite its backwoods location. And not just a few were pretty important people too, like mayors, burgesses, bank presidents, rich doctors and dentists, undertakers, barbers, sheriffs, and newspaper editors.

Important politicians stopped by when they were in the area hunting, fishing or campaigning, including Justice Jackson, Governor Martin, and the man who ran for president almost every election, Harold E. Stassen. Celebrities also; for example columnist and author, Arch Bristow (*Chicago Tribune, Erie Times*), was a regular customer and mentioned the Deerhead in several of his columns. Cartoonist Ferd Johnson, another famous Spring Creek native, dined several times at the Deerhead, and featured it several times in his world famous cartoon strip,

*Moon Mullins.* Lucille Ball was reported to have had dinner there once when visiting her home town, Jamestown, N.Y.

Eventually the Deerhead was sold to its present owners who continue to operate the Inn much as it had been for the prior half century. It remains as one of the most popular restaurants in that part of western Pennsylvania, and still draws more than its share of interesting and important people, some from long distances away.

I visit the Deerhead Inn whenever possible and shall continue to do so for as long as possible. Even though—and I am not making this up—each time I walk through the door there is a brief moment when it's not the good food and wood-burning fireplace I smell, but an unhappy little skunk who lived there about sixty years ago.

# Epilogue

It's been seventy years since the little fellow was revived by Dr. Gilly's nurse and revitalized by his Uncle Mac's moonshine. It's been about sixty years since he fought in the great garbage ambush, rescued the governor, fished in the Brokenstraw and persuaded the township farmers to vote for Alf Landon. Now, as he looks back, those sixty years shrink to a mere sixty hours. Sixty minutes! So then, how is it possible that in such a short time the Spring Creek of the 1930s is no more? How can it be the general store, feedmill, milk plant, depot, slaughterhouse, and all of the other important buildings of the 1930s have vanished without a trace? That is, all except the Congregational Church. It's still there, and looks no different than it did when visited by Apostle Paul, himself. Maybe that's the explanation why it alone still stands.

The demise of the 1930s era Spring Creek began with the advent of World War II. Eleven percent of Spring Creek's population served in the armed forces, and, as Lady Fat-emma had predicted would happen, they traveled to far off and exotic places. Most of them, unhappily not all, survived the war and returned home. However, many remained in Spring Creek just long enough to say good-bye, then returned to the outside world they'd discovered while serving their country.

At the same time, about thirty percent of Spring Creek's population obtained war-time work in one of Corry's manufacturing plants. There they learned to run or maintain machines, do clerical work, build things, and to make and spend money. When the war ended many lost their jobs but not their skills, and certainly not their desire to make and spend money. Therefore they had to leave Spring Creek to find work in cities larger and further away than Corry.

The war wasn't the only thing which put an end to the Spring Creek of the 1930s. During and after the war came better roads, a car in nearly every garage, cheaper trucks and tractors, supermarkets, shopping malls, eighteen-wheelers, refrigerated trucks, and discount houses. These things ended the need for the depot, general store, feedmill, milk plant, slaughterhouse, and blacksmith's shop.

The grade school was no longer required when busses began carrying the children to consolidated schools in neighboring cities—schools with indoor plumbing, drinking fountains, furnaces, and level fields on which to play games.

Television probably as much as anything took away the need for a community building. After all, who wants to go to an amateur talent show or Spring Bazaar or things like that when you can stay home and watch TV?

One does wonder what if there had not been a World War II; and what if bigger and better roads, cars and trucks had not been developed? What if there had been no development of shopping malls, supermarkets, and discount houses? What if TV had not been invented? Would Spring Creek still have those important buildings—at least, most of them? Might there not yet be Friday night square dances, Christmas plays, Spring Bazaars, talent shows, horseshoe pitching behind the store, and a softball game against West Spring Creek on the last day of school picnic in April?

Would Spring Creek still be a town where kids could roam much as they pleased, down to the Brokenstraw to fish, the depot to play ball in the cinder lot, and in the winter, slide down the Blue Eye Hill road? A Spring Creek where a summer day would include a game of hide and seek among the bags of grain at the feed mill; earning a nickel at the blacksmith's shop turning the handle of the "wind machine"; visiting the slaughterhouse to observe chickens, calves and cows being made into food; and a late afternoon visit to Miss Jackson's ice cream parlor for a rootbeer float?

A Spring Creek where a kid could meet and talk to politicians and learn they are people after all? And a Spring Creek where no kid could complain about not having something to do, even if it was only hanging out at Lefty's shack sneaking looks at the *Esquire* girl pictures on the wall behind Lefty's potbellied stove?